P9-DMW-648

Interactions ACCESS

LISTENING/SPEAKING

Emily Austin Thrush
Robert Baldwin
Laurie Blass

Jami Hanreddy
Listening/Speaking Strand Leader

McGraw Hill

Interactions Access Listening/Speaking, Silver Edition

Published by McGraw-Hill ESL/ELT, a business unit of The McGraw-Hill Companies, Inc., 1221 Avenue of the Americas, New York, NY 10020. Copyright © 2007 by The McGraw-Hill Companies, Inc. All rights reserved. No part of this publication may be reproduced or distributed in any form or by any means, or stored in a database or retrieval system, without the prior written consent of The McGraw-Hill Companies, Inc., including, but not limited to, in any network or other electronic storage or transmission, or broadcast for distance learning.

ISBN 13: 978-0-07-333198-0 (Student Book with Audio Highlights)
ISBN 10: 0-07-333198-8
3 4 5 6 7 8 9 10 VNH 11 10 09

Editorial director: Erik Gundersen
Series editor: Valerie Kelemen
Developmental editor: Valerie Kelemen
Production manager: Juanita Thompson
Production coordinator: Vanessa Nuttry
Cover designer: Robin Locke Monda
Interior designer: Nesbitt Graphics, Inc.
Artists: Burgundy Beam, Jonathan Massie, NETS
Photo researcher: Photoquick Research

Cover photo: Mark Andrew Kirby/Lonely Planet Images

www.esl-elt.mcgraw-hill.com
The **McGraw·Hill** Companies

A Special Thank You

The Interactions/Mosaic Silver Edition team wishes to thank our extended team: teachers, students, administrators, and teacher trainers, all of whom contributed invaluably to the making of this edition.

Macarena Aguilar, **North Harris College**, Houston, Texas ▪ Mohamad Al-Alam, **Imam Mohammad University**, Riyadh, Saudi Arabia ▪ Faisal M. Al Mohanna Abaalkhail, **King Saud University**, Riyadh, Saudi Arabia; Amal Al-Toaimy, **Women's College, Prince Sultan University**, Riyadh, Saudi Arabia ▪ Douglas Arroliga, **Ave Maria University**, Managua, Nicaragua ▪ Fairlie Atkinson, **Sungkyunkwan University**, Seoul, Korea ▪ Jose R. Bahamonde, **Miami-Dade Community College**, Miami, Florida ▪ John Ball, **Universidad de las Americas**, Mexico City, Mexico ▪ Steven Bell, **Universidad la Salle**, Mexico City, Mexico ▪ Damian Benstead, **Sungkyunkwan University**, Seoul, Korea ▪ Paul Cameron, **National Chengchi University**, Taipei, Taiwan R.O.C. ▪ Sun Chang, **Soongsil University**, Seoul, Korea ▪ Grace Chao, **Soochow University**, Taipei, Taiwan R.O.C. ▪ Chien Ping Chen, **Hua Fan University**, Taipei, Taiwan R.O.C. ▪ Selma Chen, **Chihlee Institute of Technology**, Taipei, Taiwan R.O.C. ▪ Sylvia Chiu, **Soochow University**, Taipei, Taiwan R.O.C. ▪ Mary Colonna, **Columbia University**, New York, New York ▪ Lee Culver, **Miami-Dade Community College**, Miami, Florida ▪ Joy Durighello, **City College of San Francisco**, San Francisco, California ▪ Isabel Del Valle, **Ulatina**, San Jose, Costa Rica ▪ Linda Emerson, **Sogang University**, Seoul, Korea ▪ Esther Entin, **Miami-Dade Community College**, Miami, Florida ▪ Glenn Farrier, **Gakushuin Women's College**, Tokyo, Japan ▪ Su Wei Feng, **Taipei**, Taiwan R.O.C. ▪ Judith Garcia, **Miami-Dade Community College**, Miami, Florida ▪ Maxine Gillway, **United Arab Emirates University**, Al Ain, United Arab Emirates ▪ Colin Gullberg, **Soochow University**, Taipei, Taiwan R.O.C. ▪ Natasha Haugnes, **Academy of Art University**, San Francisco, California ▪ Barbara Hockman, **City College of San Francisco**, San Francisco, California ▪ Jinyoung Hong, **Sogang University**, Seoul, Korea ▪ Sherry Hsieh, **Christ's College**, Taipei, Taiwan R.O.C. ▪ Yu-shen Hsu, **Soochow University**, Taipei, Taiwan R.O.C. ▪ Cheung Kai-Chong, **Shih-Shin University**, Taipei, Taiwan R.O.C. ▪ Leslie Kanberg, **City College of San Francisco**, San Francisco, California ▪ Gregory Keech, **City College of San Francisco**, San Francisco, California ▪ Susan Kelly, **Sogang University**, Seoul, Korea ▪ Myoungsuk Kim, **Soongsil University**, Seoul, Korea ▪ Youngsuk Kim, **Soongsil University**, Seoul, Korea ▪ Roy Langdon, **Sungkyunkwan University**, Seoul, Korea ▪ Rocio Lara, **University of Costa Rica**, San Jose, Costa Rica ▪ Insung Lee, **Soongsil University**, Seoul, Korea ▪ Andy Leung, **National Tsing Hua University**, Taipei, Taiwan R.O.C. ▪ Elisa Li Chan, **University of Costa Rica**, San Jose, Costa Rica ▪ Elizabeth Lorenzo, **Universidad Internacional de las Americas**, San Jose, Costa Rica ▪ Cheryl Magnant, **Sungkyunkwan University**, Seoul, Korea ▪ Narciso Maldonado Iuit, **Escuela Tecnica Electricista**, Mexico City, Mexico ▪ Shaun Manning, **Hankuk University of Foreign Studies**, Seoul, Korea ▪ Yoshiko Matsubayashi, **Tokyo International University**, Saitama, Japan ▪ Scott Miles, **Sogang University**, Seoul, Korea ▪ William Mooney, **Chinese Culture University**, Taipei, Taiwan R.O.C. ▪ Jeff Moore, **Sungkyunkwan University**, Seoul, Korea ▪ Mavelin de Moreno, **Lehnsen Roosevelt School**, Guatemala City, Guatemala ▪ Ahmed Motala, **University of Sharjah, Sharjah**, United Arab Emirates ▪ Carlos Navarro, **University of Costa Rica**, San Jose, Costa Rica ▪ Dan Neal, **Chih Chien University**, Taipei, Taiwan R.O.C. ▪ Margarita Novo, **University of Costa Rica**, San Jose, Costa Rica ▪ Karen O'Neill, **San Jose State University**, San Jose, California ▪ Linda O'Roke, **City College of San Francisco**, San Francisco, California ▪ Martha Padilla, **Colegio de Bachilleres de Sinaloa**, Culiacan, Mexico ▪ Allen Quesada, **University of Costa Rica**, San Jose, Costa Rica ▪ Jim Rogge, **Broward Community College**, Ft. Lauderdale, Florida ▪ Marge Ryder, **City College of San Francisco**, San Francisco, California ▪ Gerardo Salas, **University of Costa Rica**, San Jose, Costa Rica ▪ Shigeo Sato, **Tamagawa University**, Tokyo, Japan ▪ Lynn Schneider, **City College of San Francisco**, San Francisco, California ▪ Devan Scoble, **Sungkyunkwan University**, Seoul, Korea ▪ Maryjane Scott, **Soongsil University**, Seoul, Korea ▪ Ghaida Shaban, **Makassed Philanthropic School**, Beirut, Lebanon ▪ Maha Shalok, **Makassed Philanthropic School**, Beirut, Lebanon ▪ John Shannon, **University of Sharjah**, Sharjah, United Arab Emirates ▪ Elsa Sheng, **National Technology College of Taipei**, Taipei, Taiwan R.O.C. ▪ Ye-Wei Sheng, **National Taipei College of Business**, Taipei, Taiwan R.O.C. ▪ Emilia Sobaja, **University of Costa Rica**, San Jose, Costa Rica ▪ You-Souk Yoon, **Sungkyunkwan University**, Seoul, Korea ▪ Shanda Stromfield, **San Jose State University**, San Jose, California ▪ Richard Swingle, **Kansai Gaidai College**, Osaka, Japan ▪ Carol Sung, **Christ's College, Taipei**, Taiwan R.O.C. ▪ Jeng-Yih Tim Hsu, **National Kaohsiung First University of Science and Technology**, Kaohsiung, Taiwan R.O.C. ▪ Shinichiro Torikai, **Rikkyo University**, Tokyo, Japan ▪ Sungsoon Wang, **Sogang University**, Seoul, Korea ▪ Kathleen Wolf, **City College of San Francisco**, San Francisco, California ▪ Sean Wray, **Waseda University International**, Tokyo, Japan ▪ Belinda Yanda, **Academy of Art University**, San Francisco, California ▪ Su Huei Yang, **National Taipei College of Business**, Taipei, Taiwan R.O.C. ▪ Tzu Yun Yu, **Chungyu Institute of Technology**, Taipei, Taiwan R.O.C.

Photo Credits

Table of Contents

Welcome to Interactions/Mosaic Silver Edition

Interactions/Mosaic Silver Edition is a fully-integrated, 18-book academic skills series. Language proficiencies are articulated from the beginning through advanced levels <u>within</u> each of the four language skill strands. Chapter themes articulate <u>across</u> the four skill strands to systematically recycle content, vocabulary, and grammar.

NEW to the Silver Edition:

- **World's most popular and comprehensive academic skills series**—thoroughly updated for today's global learners
- **Full-color design** showcases compelling instructional photos to strengthen the educational experience
- **Enhanced focus on vocabulary building, test taking, and critical thinking skills** promotes academic achievement
- **New Self-Assessment Logs** encourage students to evaluate their learning
- **New "Best Practices" approach** promotes excellence in language teaching

NEW to Interactions Access Listening/Speaking:

- **Transparent chapter structure**—with consistent part headings, activity labeling, and clear guidance—strengthens the academic experience:
    - Part 1: Conversation
    - Part 2: Using Language
    - Part 3: Listening
    - Part 4: Speaking
- **New "Student Book with Audio Highlights"** edition allows students to personalize the learning process by listening to dialogs and pronunciation activities multiple times
- **All-new, full-color photo program** features a cast of engaging, multi-ethnic students participating in North American college life
- **New vocabulary index** offers students and instructors a chapter-by-chapter list of target words
- **Online Learning Center features MP3 files** from the Student Book audio program for students to download onto portable digital audio players

Interactions/Mosaic
Best Practices

Our Interactions/Mosaic Silver Edition team has produced an edition that focuses on Best Practices, principles that contribute to excellent language teaching and learning. Our team of writers, editors, and teacher consultants has identified the following six interconnected Best Practices:

Making Use of Academic Content

Materials and tasks based on academic content and experiences give learning real purpose. Students explore real world issues, discuss academic topics, and study content-based and thematic materials.

Organizing Information

Students learn to organize thoughts and notes through a variety of graphic organizers that accommodate diverse learning and thinking styles.

Scaffolding Instruction

A scaffold is a physical structure that facilitates construction of a building. Similarly, scaffolding instruction is a tool used to facilitate language learning in the form of predictable and flexible tasks. Some examples include oral or written modeling by the teacher or students, placing information in a larger framework, and reinterpretation.

Activating Prior Knowledge

Students can better understand new spoken or written material when they connect to the content. Activating prior knowledge allows students to tap into what they already know, building on this knowledge, and stirring a curiosity for more knowledge.

Interacting with Others

Activities that promote human interaction in pair work, small group work, and whole class activities present opportunities for real world contact and real world use of language.

Cultivating Critical Thinking

Strategies for critical thinking are taught explicitly. Students learn tools that promote critical thinking skills crucial to success in the academic world.

Highlights of Interactions Access Listening/Speaking Silver Edition

Full-color design showcases compelling instructional photos to strengthen the educational experience.

Interacting with Others
Questions and topical quotes stimulate interest, activate prior knowledge, and launch the topic of the unit.

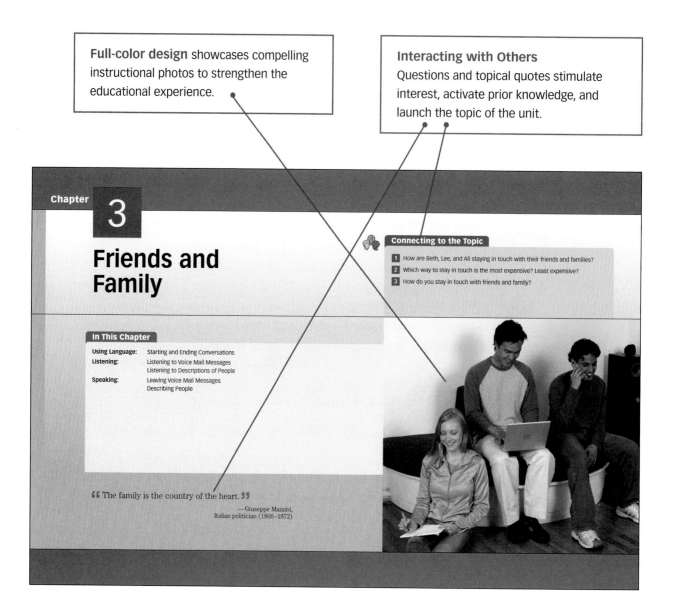

Chapter

3

Friends and Family

In This Chapter

Using Language:	Starting and Ending Conversations
Listening:	Listening to Voice Mail Messages
	Listening to Descriptions of People
Speaking:	Leaving Voice Mail Messages
	Describing People

❝ The family is the country of the heart. ❞
—Giuseppe Mazzini,
Italian politician (1805–1872)

Connecting to the Topic

1 How are Beth, Lee, and Ali staying in touch with their friends and families?
2 Which way to stay in touch is the most expensive? Least expensive?
3 How do you stay in touch with friends and family?

A student is discussing something with a parent (the student's mother or father). The student wants to pay a tutor to help him or her learn English faster. The parent wants the student to spend more time on other school subjects.

Two co-workers are discussing a problem at work. They need a new computer to help them do their work. One co-worker wants to complain to their supervisor. The other co-worker thinks the supervisor will be angry.

Part 3 Listening

Getting Meaning from Context

1 Using Context Clues You will hear a lecture about sleep in five parts. Listen to each part and choose the best answer. Continue to listen to check each answer.

1. What are you listening to?
   - (A) a conversation
   - (B) a telephone call
   - (C) a lecture in a classroom

2. What does sleep do for your brain?
   - (A) It doesn't do anything.
   - (B) It keeps your brain healthy.
   - (C) It makes you forget things.

3. Why did Carlyle Smith teach the students a list of words and a difficult problem?
   - (A) to see if they could do the problem
   - (B) to teach them English
   - (C) to test how much they remember

4. Why did Smith have the students sleep different amounts on the first, second, and third nights?
   - (A) to see if sleeping after learning helps memory
   - (B) to see if the students became angry
   - (C) to make the students sick

5. How did the students who didn't sleep much on the first or third nights remember the difficult problem?
   - (A) They remembered the same as the other students.
   - (B) They remembered better than the students who got enough sleep.
   - (C) They didn't remember the difficult problem well.

Listening to a Lecture

Before You Listen

2 Preparing to Listen Before you listen, discuss these questions with a partner.

1. When you listen to a lecture, do you take notes? What information do you try to write down?
2. Do you review your notes before taking a test?
3. Do you try to sleep well before a test or do you stay up late studying?

> **Strategy**
>
> **Using a Flow Chart**
> A graphic organizer called a *flow chart* can help you organize the steps in a process. Each step is a section of the flow chart. You will practice making a flow chart in Activity 3.

3 Thinking About Taking Notes and Passing Tests Fill in the flow chart below. What should a student do to get good grades? Start with "Arrive to the lecture on time (or 5 minutes early)" and end with "Take the test." When you finish, compare your charts with the rest of the class.

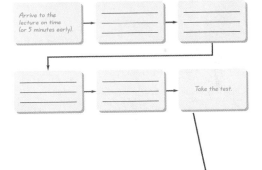

Activating Prior Knowledge
Pre-listening activities place the lecture, academic discussion, or conversation in context and allow the student to listen actively.

Enhanced focus on vocabulary building promotes academic achievement.

Part 1 Conversation: Looking for a Summer Job

Before You Listen

 1 **Prelistening Questions** Ask and answer these questions with a small group.

1. Look at the photos below. Describe each job.
2. Which of these jobs would you like to have? Why?
3. What job(s) would you like to do in the future? Why?

▲ Financial analyst looking at a chart   ▲ Architects discussing a project

 2 **Vocabulary Preview** Ali and Alicia are at the Faber College Career Planning and Placement Center. They are at the job board looking for summer jobs. Listen to these words from their conversation. Check (✓) the words that you know.

Nouns	Verbs	Adjectives
❑ (one's) company	❑ find out	❑ full-time
❑ experience	❑ look for	❑ part-time
❑ journalism		
❑ public health		**Expression**
❑ reporter		❑ Don't mention it.

3 **Guessing the Meanings of New Words from Context** Guess the meanings of the underlined words. Write your guesses on the lines. Check your answers with a dictionary or with your teacher.

1. Lee worked last summer for a computer software company. He got a lot of good <u>experience</u> in programming and designing computer games.

   My guess: _____

2. There are many ways to <u>find out</u> what jobs are available. You can read the paper, look on the Internet, call local companies, or ask people you know.

   My guess: _____

3. Thousands of people in my city became sick with the flu last year. This was a <u>public health</u> problem, so the government and the doctors worked together to solve the problem.

   My guess: _____

4. Mina is unhappy with her current job. She will <u>look for</u> a job where she can work with children.

   My guess: _____

5. After the plane crash, the <u>reporter</u> had to interview the families of the passengers and then write a story about them for the newspaper.

   My guess: _____

6. Ali is still in school, so he doesn't have time for a <u>full-time</u> job. He wants a <u>part-time</u> job for about 20 hours a week.

   My guess (full-time): _____

   My guess (part-time): _____

7. Alicia is studying <u>journalism</u>. She wants to work for a newspaper or a TV news show.

   My guess: _____

8. Ali and Alicia like to do things together. They enjoy each other's <u>company</u>.

   My guess: _____

9. **Lee:** Thanks for helping me with my homework, Beth.

   Beth: <u>Don't mention it</u>!

   My guess: _____

Scaffolding Instruction

Instruction and practice build gradually to support students in the listening tasks.

Cultivating Critical Thinking

Critical thinking strategies and activities equip students with the skills they need for academic achievement.

Listen

4 Listening for Main Ideas (Part 1) Listen to the first part of the conversation. Choose the best answer to each question.

1. What are Dan, Beth, and Ali enjoying?
   - (A) visiting San Francisco
   - (B) looking at the San Francisco skyline
   - (C) the tour of Alcatraz

2. What is the Transamerica Building?
   - (A) a San Francisco landmark and part of the San Francisco skyline
   - (B) a triangular tower
   - (C) both a and b

3. What is Alcatraz?
   - (A) a prison where dangerous criminals are put
   - (B) a former prison and an interesting place to tour
   - (C) a famous bridge

5 Listening for Main Ideas (Part 2) Now listen to the whole conversation. Choose the best answer to each question.

1. What does Dan say he wants to do tomorrow?
   - (A) visit Alcatraz
   - (B) see all of San Francisco's famous landmarks
   - (C) change the flat tire

2. Why does Dan pull the car over?
   - (A) because the car has a flat tire
   - (B) because they (Dan, Beth, and Ali) need to get to San Francisco
   - (C) because they want to visit Alcatraz

3. What does Ali say about the flat tire?
   - (A) It will take a long time to change it.
   - (B) It will take a short time to change it.
   - (C) Dan and Beth can change it.

▲ Beth

▲ Ali

▲ Dan

6 Listening for Specific Information Listen again. Choose best answer to each question.

1. Ali says, "I can't wait to go to all those places". What does he mean?
   - (A) He's excited about visiting San Francisco's famous landmarks.
   - (B) He's going to visit San Francisco's famous landmarks today.
   - (C) He wants to visit just Alcatraz.

2. What does Dan want to do tomorrow?
   - (A) visit Alcatraz all day
   - (B) visit Alcatraz, perhaps in the morning or the afternoon
   - (C) visit all of San Francisco's landmarks

3. How long will it take to change the flat tire?
   - (A) A few minutes
   - (B) All afternoon
   - (C) A day

After You Listen

Strategy

Using a Graphic Organizer: T-charts

To compare two things, you can make a graphic organizer called a T-chart. For example, you can compare two places by using a T-chart. Label one column with one place and the other column with the other place. Write words describing each place below the labels. Group the negative words and the positive words. A T-chart can help you choose which place is better. The T-chart below compares two places: the beach and the mountains. You will practice making a T-chart to compare two places in Activity 7.

The Beach	The Mountains
warm	cold
sand	snow
water	ice
vacation place	vacation place
swimming	skiing
bathing suit	coat

Enhanced focus on test taking skills

promotes academic achievement.

Scope and Sequence

Chapter	Listening	Speaking	Critical Thinking
1 Neighborhoods, Cities, and Towns page 2	■ Listening for main ideas ■ Listening for specific information ■ Using context clues	■ Asking for and giving personal information ■ Confirming information ■ Talking about days and dates ■ Talking about cities and transportation	■ Comparing and contrasting ■ Interpreting a photo ■ Using a Venn diagram to compare and contrast ■ Evaluating search engines and keywords
2 Shopping and E-Commerce page 26	■ Listening for prices ■ Listening to online shopping information ■ Listening for reasons ■ Listening for reductions	■ Comparing prices and stores ■ Describing clothes ■ Interviewing classmates about shopping habits ■ Role play: returning merchandise to a store ■ Giving reasons	■ Developing reasoning skills for argumentation ■ Interpreting information on shopping websites ■ Using charts to compare and contrast
3 Friends and Family page 50	■ Listening for conversation starters ■ Listening to voice mail messages ■ Listening to descriptions of people ■ Listening for reductions	■ Describing people ■ Leaving voice mail messages ■ Interviewing classmates about friends and ways to keep in touch ■ Role play: appropriate greetings based on situations	■ Analyzing appropriate and inappropriate topics of conversation ■ Problem-solving: leaving appropriate voice mail messages
4 Health Care page 70	■ Listening for main ideas ■ Listening for specific information ■ Listening for advice ■ Listening to instructions ■ Listening to complaints ■ Using context clues	■ Discussing solutions to health problems ■ Giving advice ■ Discussing complaints ■ Discussing health advice and habits ■ Talking about body parts	■ Analyzing solutions to problems ■ Making comparisons ■ Interpreting photos ■ Using charts to organize information

Vocabulary Building	Pronunciation	Language Skills
■ Neighborhood terms ■ Time and distance terms ■ Expressions about fares ■ Guessing meaning from context ■ Practicing new words in a variety of contexts	■ Listening for and using stress	■ Understanding large numbers ■ Using prepositions with days and dates ■ Using contractions
■ Shopping terms ■ Price expressions ■ Clothing types and colors ■ Guessing meaning from context	■ Using reductions ■ Listening for and using stressed words	■ Describing clothing ■ Using monetary terms for prices
■ Expressions for describing people ■ Expressions for starting and ending conversations ■ Guessing meaning from context	■ Listening for and using stressed words	■ Starting and ending conversations: formal vs. informal language ■ Topics of conversation
■ Words and expressions for discussing health care ■ Words and expressions for making health care appointments ■ Guessing meaning from context ■ Body part terms	■ Listening for and using stressed words ■ Listening for reductions ■ Using online pronouncing dictionaries	■ Using modals to give advice

Vocabulary Building	Pronunciation	Language Skills
■ Words and expressions for discussing male and female relationships ■ Dating and social event terms ■ Guessing meaning from context	■ Listening for and using stressed words	■ Patterns for small talk
■ Expressions for agreeing and disagreeing ■ Understanding basic vocabulary used in research studies ■ Transition vocabulary for narratives ■ Guessing meaning from context	■ Stress: teens and tens ■ Listening for and using stressed words	■ Polite and impolite ways to agree and disagree
■ Words and expressions for discussing jobs and careers ■ Job titles and major terms ■ Job interview terms ■ Guessing meaning from context	■ Listening for and using stressed words ■ Distinguishing majors and job titles	■ Making complaints
■ Words and expressions for discussing food and nutrition ■ Guessing meaning from context ■ Words and expressions for giving a sequence	■ Listening for and using stressed words	■ Using sequencing words ■ Using present tense to talk about food preferences

Vocabulary Building	Pronunciation	Language Skills
■ Describing places and events ■ Travel terms ■ Guessing meaning from context	■ Listening for and using stressed words	■ Using modals and expressions to persuade ■ Using past tense to talk about travel
■ Words and expressions for discussing the environment and endangered species ■ Terms of persuasion ■ Guessing meaning from context	■ Listening for and using stressed words ■ Using stressed words for emphasis	■ Using present tense to agree and disagree ■ Using the imperative to give advice

Name: **Ali**
Nationality: **American**

Name: **Beth**
Nationality: **American**

Name: **Lee**
Nationality: **Korean**

Name: **Alicia**
Nationality: **Mexican**

Name: Ming
Nationality: Chinese

Name: Dan
Nationality: American

Name: Peter
Nationality: Puerto Rican

Name: Michel
Nationality: French

1

Neighborhoods, Cities, and Towns

ff What is the city but the people? "

—William Shakespeare,
English playwright (1564–1616)

Connecting to the Topic

1. Beth, Ali, and Lee are students at Faber College. Do you think Faber College is in a big city or a small town? Why?

2. Where are Beth, Ali, and Lee? What are they doing?

3. What do you think Beth, Ali, and Lee will do next?

Before You Listen

1 Discussing Cities and Towns Look at these photos. Talk to a classmate. Compare and contrast the two places. Use the chart below to help you with your discussion.

▲ A city

▲ A town

Features	A City	A Town
Buildings: Tall? Low?		
Traffic: Light? Heavy?		
People: Few/Not crowded? Many/Crowded?		
Air: Clean? Polluted (dirty)?		
Lifestyle: Quiet? Noisy? Exciting? Busy?		
Transportation: Private cars? Public buses? Taxis?		

2 **Vocabulary Preview** Listen to these words and expressions from Ali, Beth, and Lee's conversation. Check (✓) the words and expressions that you know.

Nouns	**Adjective**	**Expression**
❏ capital	❏ interesting	❏ Are you kidding?
❏ hometown		
❏ nightlife		
❏ population		
❏ transportation		

3 **Guessing the Meanings of New Words from Context** Guess the meanings of the underlined words and expressions. Write your guesses on the lines. Check your answers with a dictionary or with your teacher.

1. Life in a big city is always <u>interesting</u>. There are a lot of things to do.

   My guess: _____

2. What kind of <u>transportation</u> do you use—the train, the bus, or the subway?

   My guess: _____

3. My <u>hometown</u> is Mexico City. I was born there, and I still live there.

   My guess: _____

4. Paris is the <u>capital</u> of France. The government offices are there.

   My guess: _____

5. Seoul, Korea, has a large <u>population</u>. More than ten million people live there.

   My guess: _____

6. New York has fantastic <u>nightlife</u>. There are clubs, discos, and other places to have fun at night.

   My guess: _____

7. **A:** Is there any good nightlife in New York?

   B: <u>Are you kidding</u>? There's fantastic nightlife in New York!

   My guess: _____

▲ Mexico City

▲ Paris

▲ Seoul

Listen

 4 **Listening for Main Ideas** Listen to the first part of the conversation and choose the best answer to each question.

1. What is Beth doing?
- (A) She's meeting Ali for the first time.
- (B) She's meeting Lee for the first time.
- (C) She's meeting her friends, Ali and Lee.

2. What is Seoul?
- (A) Beth's hometown
- (B) the capital of Korea
- (C) a small town in northern California

3. What is San Anselmo, California?
- (A) Lee's hometown
- (B) a capital city
- (C) a small town

 5 **Listening for Specific Information** Listen to the complete conversation and choose the best answer to each question.

1. Who is Beth?
- (A) Lee's friend
- (B) Ali's friend
- (C) Ali's cousin

2. What is the population of Seoul?
- (A) less than 100,000
- (B) between 1,000,000 and 2,000,000
- (C) more than 10,000,000

3. What does Lee say about Seoul?
- (A) It's a small city.
- (B) There isn't any good public transportation.
- (C) There are hundreds of clubs and discos there.

4. Why does Lee say Seoul has "fantastic nightlife"?
- (A) because it's a big city
- (B) because there are a lot of people
- (C) because there are hundreds of clubs and discos

After You Listen

6 **Vocabulary Review** Complete the sentences. Use words from the box.

capital	interesting	nightlife	transportation
hometown	kidding	population	

1. Seoul is the _____ of Korea.

2. There's good public _____ in Seoul. It's easy to get around.

3. Seoul has a large _____. Over ten million people live there.

4. I'm from San Anselmo, California. What's your _____?

5. My classes are _____. I'm really enjoying them and learning a lot.

6. The _____ in Tokyo is fantastic. There are clubs, restaurants, and shows in the evening.

7. **A:** Would you like to go to Paris?

   B: Are you _____? I'd love to go!

Stress

STRESSING WORDS IN ENGLISH

In English conversation, some words are *stressed*. That is, we say these stressed words louder and clearer than other words. Words can be stressed for several reasons. It is important for speaking and listening comprehension to understand this pattern of speaking in English.

Example

′		′	
Nice	to	meet	you.
(stressed)		(stressed)	

In this book, you will practice listening for stress.

7 Listening for Stressed Words Listen to the first part of the conversation again. The stressed words are marked.

Ali: Beth! Hey, Beth! How's it going?

Beth: Ali! Hi! I'm fine. How're you?

Ali: Fine, thanks. Beth, this is Lee. Lee, this is my friend, Beth.

Lee: Nice to meet you.

Beth: Nice to meet you. Are you from around here?

Lee: No. I'm from Seoul, Korea.

Beth: Really? That's interesting. Seoul's the capital of Korea, isn't it?

Lee: Yes, that's right. How about you? What's your hometown?

Contractions

COMBINING WORDS WITH CONTRACTIONS

Contractions are a way to combine words. When you put the two words together, you drop letters and replace those letters with an apostrophe ('). People use contractions in speaking and in writing.

Long Form	Contraction
I am from Seoul.	**I'm** from Seoul.
Seoul is the capital.	**Seoul's** the capital.
It is a really big city.	**It's** a really big city.

8 **Comparing Long Forms and Contractions** Listen to the following sentences from the conversation. Repeat the sentences after the speaker.

Long Form	Contraction
1. How is it going?	How's it going?
2. I am fine.	I'm fine.
3. Seoul is the capital.	Seoul's the capital.
4. It is a really big city.	It's a really big city.
5. That is a lot of people!	That's a lot of people!
6. There is good public transportation.	There's good public transportation.

9 **Listening for Contractions** Listen to the sentences. Circle the letter of the sentence that you hear.

1. a. I am fine.   b. I'm fine.

2. a. He is from Seoul.   b. He's from Seoul.

3. a. It is the capital of Korea.   b. It's the capital of Korea.

4. a. There is great nightlife there.   b. There's great nightlife there.

5. a. What is the population?   b. What's the population?

Using the Internet

Using Search Engines and Keywords

You can use the Internet to practice listening and speaking. To find websites, use a search engine such as www.google.com. Use *keywords* to find websites about a specific topic. Keywords are words that are related to your topic. For example, if you want to find information about English language learning sites that have pronunciation practice, you can use the keywords *English* and *pronunciation* to get a list of useful websites.

To start a search, go to a search engine. Type your keyword(s) into the text box. Then, click the Submit or Search button.

| English pronunciation | | **Submit** |

The search engine will show you a list of websites on your topic. Click on a choice to see a website.

Note: To practice pronunciation or listening on the Internet, make sure you have headphones or speakers.

10 **Practicing Your Search Skills** List possible keywords to do searches for the topics below.

- practicing English pronunciation ⎯⎯⎯⎯⎯⎯⎯⎯⎯⎯⎯⎯⎯⎯⎯⎯
- practicing English contractions ⎯⎯⎯⎯⎯⎯⎯⎯⎯⎯⎯⎯⎯⎯⎯⎯
- practicing English stress ⎯⎯⎯⎯⎯⎯⎯⎯⎯⎯⎯⎯⎯⎯⎯⎯⎯⎯
- your own idea ⎯⎯⎯⎯⎯⎯⎯⎯⎯⎯⎯⎯⎯⎯⎯⎯⎯⎯⎯⎯⎯⎯

Now, choose one of the topics above. Open a search engine such as www.google.com. Use the keywords from your list to find three websites on your topic. Report to the class on your search.

1. Which topic did you choose?

2. Which keywords did you use?

3. Did you find useful websites?

4. Which websites were useful?

Talk It Over

11 Getting to Know You

1. Work in groups of four. Each person in the group should choose a different role-play card from page 11 and read it. You will answer questions about the information on your card.

2. Write your teacher's name and the names of your group members in the spaces at the top of the chart.

3. Look at the example (Stacy).

   Example　**A:** What's your name?

   　　　　　　B: Stacy.

   　　　　　　A: Where are you from?

   　　　　　　B: I'm from Kansas City.

4. Write your own question for item number 7.

5. As a class, practice asking your teacher the questions and write his or her answers on the chart.

6. Take turns asking your group members the questions. Write their answers on the chart.

Question	Name	Teacher	Name	Name	Name
	Stacy				
1. Where are you from?	*Kansas City*				
2. What country is your hometown in?	*United States*				
3. Is your hometown small, medium-sized, or big?	*Medium-sized*				
4. What's the population?	*441, 545*				
5. Is there good public transportation?	*Yes*				
6. Is there good nightlife? Give an example.	*Yes, many clubs*				
7. Your question:					

City: Kyoto
Country: Japan
Small, medium-sized, or big: Big
Population: 1,461,140
Public transportation: Yes
Nightlife: many clubs and
karaoke bars

City: Curitiba
Country: Brazil
Small, medium-sized, or big: Big
Population: 1,465,698
Public transportation: Yes
Nightlife: many clubs for dancing

City: Puebla
Country: Mexico
Small, medium-sized, or big: Big
Population: 1,400,000
Public transportation: Yes
Nightlife: many discos and bars

City: Chiang Mai
Country: Thailand
Small, medium-sized, or big:
Medium-sized
Population: 164,902
Public transportation: Yes
Nightlife: many clubs with live music

▲ Night in the streets of Tokyo's Shibuya District

Asking for and Giving Personal Information

WHEN SOMEONE ASKS FOR YOUR PERSONAL INFORMATION

Sometimes you must give your personal information (name, address, telephone number, email address). Examples include:

- to a new friend
- to a company that is mailing something to you
- when you are registering for classes

Example

A: What is your name and address?

B: Jamie Burns,
231 Ellsworth Street,
San Francisco, CA,
94933

Sometimes you *don't* want to give your personal information. Examples include:

- at a party
- to a stranger on the street

▲ What is your name and address?

Here are some things that you can say when you don't want to give your personal information.

Example

A: What's your phone number?

B: I'd rather not say.
or
I'm afraid I don't give out my address and phone number.
or
I'm sorry, I don't give out personal information.

▲ What's your phone number?

1 **Listening for Personal Information** Listen to the conversation. Write the information that you hear. If the person doesn't give personal information, write *X*.

1. First name: _____Gordon_____ Last name: _____McKay_____
   Address: __X__ _____East Park Avenue, Apartment_____ __1__
   Telephone number: _____

2. First name: _____ Last name: _____
   Address: _____ _____Southern Avenue_____
   Telephone number: _____
   Fax number: _____

3. First name: _____ Last name: _____
   Address: _____P.O. Box_____ _____ _____Shing Wong Street, Hong Kong_____
   Telephone number: _____
   Email address: _____

4. First name: _____ Last name: _____
   Telephone number: _____

2 **Writing Personal Information** Write information about yourself.

First name: _____

Last name: _____

Address: _____

_____

Telephone number: _____

Fax number: _____

Email address: _____

3 **Writing Personal Information Questions** Work with a partner. Write six personal information questions on a piece of paper.

Example What is your name?

Confirming Information

Sometimes you are not sure that you heard personal information correctly. If you are not sure, you can repeat the information as a question.

Example

Ms. Dunn:	What's your telephone number?
Gordon McKay:	My number is 555-7950.
Ms. Dunn:	555-7950?
Gordon McKay:	That's right.

4 Asking for and Confirming Personal Information Move around the room. Ask your classmates the questions that you wrote in Activity 3. Write down the names, addresses, telephone numbers, fax numbers, and email addresses of some of your classmates. To make sure that you heard the information correctly, repeat it as a question. If you don't want to give personal information, use one of the expressions in the box on page 12.

Part 3 Listening

Getting Meaning from Context

Before You Listen

1 Prelistening Questions Discuss these questions with your class.

1. What do you think is the largest city in the world (in population)?

2. How many people do you think live in the world's largest city?

3. How much is the airfare from your hometown to a major city such as New York, London, or Paris?

4. How do you get to school every day?

5. Do you like the way you get to school? Why or why not?

Listen

2 **Using Context Clues** You will hear five conversations. Listen to each conversation and choose the best answer. Continue to listen to check each answer.

1. What is Mexico City like?
- Ⓐ It's a small town.
- Ⓑ It's a very small city.
- Ⓒ It's a very large city.

2. Why isn't Lee going home for New Year's?
- Ⓐ because Seoul is far away
- Ⓑ because there aren't any flights
- Ⓒ because it costs too much money

3. How will the man go to Central Avenue?
- Ⓐ He'll go by bus.
- Ⓑ He'll walk.
- Ⓒ He'll go by car.

4. Why doesn't Beth take the subway?
- Ⓐ It's too crowded.
- Ⓑ It's not fast enough.
- Ⓒ It doesn't go to the university.

5. What does Ali like about his new place to live?
- Ⓐ It's really small.
- Ⓑ It's really old.
- Ⓒ It's close to school.

Before You Listen

Strategy

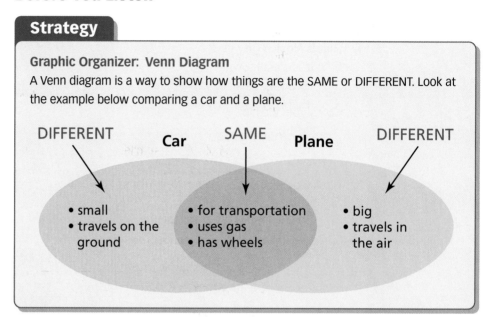

Graphic Organizer: Venn Diagram

A Venn diagram is a way to show how things are the SAME or DIFFERENT. Look at the example below comparing a car and a plane.

DIFFERENT   **Car**   SAME   **Plane**   DIFFERENT

- small
- travels on the ground

- for transportation
- uses gas
- has wheels

- big
- travels in the air

 3 **Using a Venn Diagram** Write the names of two kinds of transportation you and your partner use most above each circle below. With your partner, decide how these forms are the same and how they are different. Complete the Venn diagram.

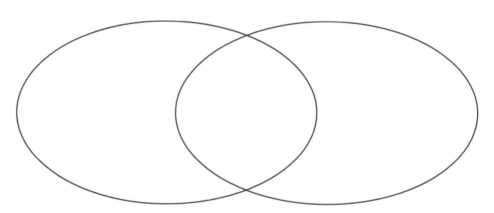

 4 **Vocabulary Preview** Listen to these time and distance words. Check (✓) the ones that you know.

Time

❏ a minute	❏ two minutes	❏ a two-minute ride/walk
❏ an hour	❏ two hours	❏ a two-hour ride/walk
	❏ half an hour	❏ a half-hour ride/walk

Distance

❏ a mile	❏ two miles	❏ a two-mile ride/walk

FYI

One mile is 1.6 kilometers.

Listen

5 Listening for Main Ideas Listen and answer these questions about the conversation.

1. How does the man get to school? _____

2. How does the woman get to school? _____

6 Listening for Specific Information Listen again. Complete the conversation with words from the box.

fifteen-minute	one mile	ten miles	thirty minutes	three-hour

Woman: So, how do you get to school every day?

Man: I take the subway. It's fast.

Woman: You don't take the bus?

Man: Nah, the bus is too slow. It takes _____

1
to get to school from my place.

Woman: Yeah, I know what you mean.

Man: How 'bout you?

Woman: Oh, I walk. My apartment's close. About _____

2
from school. It's just a _____ walk.

3

Man: Wow, that's great. My place is far from school—about
_____. So I can't walk . . .

4

Woman: Yeah, that's about a _____ walk!

5

After You Listen

7 Discussing Time and Distance Talk about the answers to these questions in small groups.

1. How far is your home from school in miles? In kilometers?

2. How long does it take you to get to school?

3. What is the best way for you to get to school?

4. Why is this the best way for you to get to school? Is it fast? Cheap?

Before You Listen

 8 Prelistening Questions Before you listen, look at the photos and discuss the questions below with a partner.

▲ A ferry

▲ An elevated railway

1. What kinds of public transportation do you have in your town or city? Check (✓) them.

   _____ bus

   _____ subway

   _____ ferry

   _____ elevated railway

   _____ train

   _____ other: _____

2. What do you like about the public transportation in your city?

3. What do you dislike (not like)?

 9 Vocabulary Preview Listen to these words and expressions about fares. Check (✓) the ones that you know.

Nouns	Verb	Adjective	Expression
❑ exact change	❑ divided	❑ good for	❑ in advance
❑ fare			
❑ pass			
❑ public transportation			
❑ seniors			
❑ ticket			
❑ zone			

Listen

10 Listening for Main Ideas Now listen to the information about public transportation in Vancouver, Canada. Complete the activity.

What kinds of public transportation are there in Vancouver? Check (✓) them.

_____ bus

_____ subway

_____ ferry

_____ elevated railway

_____ train

11 Listening for Specific Information (Part 1) Listen again and complete the chart with the regular zone fares.

Zones	Adults	Seniors, Students, and Children
1 Zone		
2 Zones		
3 Zones		

12 Listening for Specific Information (Part 2) Listen a third time. This time fill in the blanks with special prices and day pass prices.

1. Evenings, weekends, and holidays: _____

2. Day pass for adults: _____

3. Day pass for children: _____

After You Listen

13 Discussing Public Transportation Information Answer these questions in small groups.

1. Do you have transportation zones in your city or town?

2. Do you have special fares in your city or town? For seniors? For children? For students?

3. Do most people in your city or town buy daily fares or monthly passes?

4. Which is better: a daily fare or a monthly pass? Why?

5. Which kind of public transportation do you like best? Why?

6. Is the public transportation in your city or town easy to use for visitors or tourists? Why or why not?

Talking About Days and Dates

WRITING AND SAYING DATES

Cardinal numbers are 1, 2, 3, 4, 5, 6, 7 . . .

Ordinal numbers tell about order. Ordinal numbers are 1st, 2nd, 3rd, 4th, 5th, 6th, 7th . . .

Write dates as cardinal or ordinal numbers. Say dates as ordinal numbers.

Examples

Write	**Say**
June 1 (or June 1st)	June first
Aug. 14 (or Aug. 14th)	August fourteenth

▲ "It's Saturday, March ninth."

1 **Saying Months** Practice saying these words with your teacher.

January	May	September
February	June	October
March	July	November
April	August	December

2 **Saying Dates** Practice saying these dates with your teacher.

Example Oct. 18 (Oct. 18th)

Say "October eighteenth."

1. Jan. 2 (Jan. 2nd)

2. Dec. 3 (Dec. 3rd)

3. Feb. 1 (Feb. 1st)

4. Aug. 25 (Aug. 25th)

5. Nov. 15 (Nov. 15th)

6. Sept. 30 (Sept. 30th)

PREPOSITIONS AND DATES

Use *in* and *on* before dates. Use *in* to talk about a month or year. Use *on* to talk about a specific date.

Examples

New Year's Day is **in** January.
New Year's Day is **on** January 1.

---

3 **Using *In* or *On* for Dates** Write *in* or *on* for each sentence.

1. School starts _____ September.

2. School starts _____ September 6.

3. The exam is _____ February.

4. The exam is _____ February 13th.

5. Elizabeth's birthday is _____ August.

6. Elizabeth's birthday is _____ August 23rd.

4 **Talking About Days and Dates**

1. Work with a partner. Student A looks at Calendar A on page 22. Student B looks at Calendar B on page 23.

2. Student A asks questions about the events listed in the box below Calendar A. For example, Student A asks, "When is Stacy's birthday?" Student B looks at Calendar B and says, "Stacy's birthday is on May 13."

3. Student A then writes "Stacy's birthday" on the May 13 square.

4. After Student A finishes asking questions, Student B asks questions and Student A listens and answers. Student B fills in Calendar B.

5. When you finish, compare your calendars. Both calendars should have the same information.

◄ Stacy's birthday
is on May 13.

Calendar A—May

Sunday	Monday	Tuesday	Wednesday	Thursday	Friday	Saturday
	1	2	3	4	5	6
7	8	9	10	11	12 grammar test	13 *Stacy's birthday*
14 jazz festival	15	16	17	18	19	20 basketball game
21	22	23	24	25	26 doctor's appointment	27
28 art show	29	30	31			

1. Stacy's birthday   **3.** dentist's appointment   **5.** tennis match

2. final exam   **4.** concert   **6.** school picnic

Self-Assessment Log

Check the words and expressions that you learned in this chapter.

Nouns	Verb	Adjectives	Expressions
❏ capital	❏ divided	❏ good for	❏ Are you kidding?
❏ exact change		❏ interesting	❏ in advance
❏ fare			
❏ hometown			
❏ nightlife			
❏ pass			
❏ population			
❏ public transportation			
❏ seniors			
❏ ticket			
❏ transportation			
❏ zone			

Check the things that you did in this chapter. How well can you do each one?

	Very well	Fairly well	Not very well
I can listen for the main ideas.	❏	❏	❏
I can listen for specific information.	❏	❏	❏
I can guess the meanings of words from context.	❏	❏	❏
I can listen for stress and contractions.	❏	❏	❏
I can search the Internet.	❏	❏	❏
I can ask for and give personal information.	❏	❏	❏
I can confirm information.	❏	❏	❏
I can use a Venn diagram to compare things.	❏	❏	❏
I can talk about days and dates.	❏	❏	❏
I can talk about transportation.	❏	❏	❏

Write about what you learned and what you did in this chapter.

In this chapter,

I learned _____

_____

I liked _____

_____

2

Shopping and E-Commerce

> " If you can't smile, don't open a store. "
>
> —Chinese proverb

Connecting to the Topic

1 Where are Ali, Beth, and Alicia? What do you think they are doing?

2 Where do you like to shop? What do you like to shop for?

3 Do you shop online? What do you buy online?

Before You Listen

1 **Comparing Online Shopping to Traditional Shopping** Look at these photos. How are the two ways of shopping different? How are they similar? Talk to a classmate. Use the chart below to help with your discussion.

▲ Shopping in a store

▲ Shopping online

Features	Shopping in a Store	Shopping Online
Where: Indoors? Outdoors?		
When: Anytime? Only during store hours?		
What do you need to shop?: A car or other transportation? A computer? An Internet account (like AOL)?		
How do you shop?: Talk to a salesperson? Give personal information? Try (on) a product before buying? Window-shop (browse) without buying anything?		
How can you pay?: By cash? By credit card? By ATM (bank) card? By personal check? By traveler's check?		

2 **Prelistening Questions** Look at the photo. Ali and Beth are at Alicia's apartment. Alicia is also a student at Faber College. Answer the questions with a classmate.

1. Alicia just opened her apartment door. What do you think Alicia says to Ali and Beth?

2. What do you think Beth says to Alicia?

3. Alicia doesn't know Ali. What is Beth saying to introduce Alicia and Ali?

4. Why do you think Beth and Ali are at Alicia's apartment?

 3 **Vocabulary Preview** Listen to these words and expressions from Ali, Beth, and Alicia's conversation. Check (✓) the words and expressions that you know.

Noun
- ❏ mall

Verbs
- ❏ browse
- ❏ look around
- ❏ look for (parking)
- ❏ save money/time/energy/gas
- ❏ spend money/time
- ❏ try (on)

Adjective
- ❏ crowded

Expression
- ❏ No problem

4 **Guessing the Meanings of New Words from Context** Guess the meanings of the underlined words. Write your guesses on the lines. Check your answers with a dictionary or your teacher.

1. Too many people shop at this place—this store is too <u>crowded</u>!

   My guess: _____

2. Alicia can <u>save</u> gas if she doesn't drive her car.

   My guess: _____

3. I like to shop at the <u>mall</u> because there are a lot of different stores there.

   My guess: _____

4. The parking garage is full, so Ali is going to <u>look for</u> parking on the street.

   My guess: _____

5. I can't go shopping because I can't <u>spend</u> any money.

   My guess: _____

6. Beth and Ali don't have any money, so they're just going to <u>look around</u> in some stores and not buy anything.

   My guess: _____

7. Alicia is going to <u>try on</u> the dress to see if it's the right size.

   My guess: _____

8. Alicia likes to <u>browse</u>—sometimes it's fun to look but not buy anything.

   My guess: _____

9. **A:** Can I try on this dress?

   B: Sure, <u>no problem</u>!

   My guess: _____

Listen

5 **Listening for Main Ideas (Part 1)** Listen to the first part of the conversation. Choose the best answer to each question.

1. Where are Beth and Ali?
   - Ⓐ They're at Beth's apartment.
   - Ⓑ They're at a store.
   - Ⓒ They're at Alicia's apartment.

2. Beth introduces Ali to Alicia. Then, what do Beth, Ali, and Alicia do?
   - Ⓐ They come in to Alicia's apartment.
   - Ⓑ They have some coffee and soda.
   - Ⓒ They go shopping.

3. What kind of shopping does Alicia usually do?

(A) She doesn't know.

(B) She goes window-shopping with Beth.

(C) She shops online.

6 Listening for Main Ideas (Part 2) Now listen to the whole conversation. Choose the best answer to each question.

1. Why does Alicia like online shopping?

(A) The clothes are cheaper.

(B) It saves time.

(C) She can try on clothes.

2. What do Beth and Ali dislike (not like) about online shopping?

(A) They have to drive and look for parking.

(B) It's so crowded these days.

(C) They can't touch and try on things they want to buy.

3. What are Beth, Ali, and Alicia going to do?

(A) They're going to stay at Alicia's apartment and shop online.

(B) They're going to go shopping at a mall and spend some money.

(C) They're going to go window-shopping and not spend any money.

7 Listening for Specific Information Listen again. Choose the best answer to each question.

1. Beth introduces Alicia to Ali. Alicia says, "It's nice to meet you." What does Ali say?

(A) "How are you?"

(B) "Nice to meet you, too."

(C) "Nice meeting you."

2. What does Alicia offer Beth and Ali?

(A) coffee or soda

(B) water or tea

(C) water and a seat

3. Ali asks Alicia, "Why do you want to sit in front of a computer screen?" Why does he ask this?

(A) because it's a nice day

(B) because Ali wants Alicia to go window shopping

(C) both a and b

Strategy

Graphic Organizer: Compare and Contrast Chart
A compare and contrast chart is a good way to look at the good (pro) and bad (con) points of two or more subjects. Look at the example below comparing bicycles and cars.

	Pro	Con
Bicycles	clean good exercise cheap	slow
Cars	fast	make air dirty expensive

 8 **Using a Compare and Contrast Chart to Understand Main Ideas**
What do Beth, Ali, and Alicia say about shopping in a store and shopping online? Fill in the chart below with a partner. Add your ideas. Then share your ideas with the class.

	Pro	Con
Shopping in a Store		
Shopping Online	*saves time*	

9 Vocabulary Review Complete the sentences below. Use words from the box. Some words may be used more than once. Some sentences have two possible answers.

browse	look for	online shopping	try on
crowded	mall	save	
look around	no problem	spend	

1. Do you want to buy something at the mall or do you just want to

   _____?

2. I'm going to the mall just to _____; I'm not going to buy anything.

3. _____ is easy, but you need a computer.

4. We want to shop for three different things, so let's go to the

   _____.

5. Ali needs to _____ parking before he can go into the mall.

6. I don't have a lot of money, so I don't want to _____ it.

7. Alicia likes to _____ time. She does a lot of online shopping because it's fast.

8. Beth wants to _____ these pants before she buys them.

9. This store is so _____! I don't like it when there are so many people.

10. **A:** I'd like to try on these pants.

    B: Okay, _____!

Stress

10 Listening for Stressed Words Listen to a part of the conversation again. The words in the box below are stressed. Fill in the blanks with the words from the box. Some words may be used more than once.

Ali	good	meet	seat
doing	How	nice	Thanks
in	please	too	

Alicia: Hi, Beth. Come on _____.
                                          1

Beth: Hi, Alicia! _____ are you _____?
                                    2   3

Alicia: Pretty _____.
                              4

Beth: Alicia, this is my friend _____. He's from Silver Spring, Maryland.

5

Alicia: Hi, Ali. It's _____ to _____ you.

6 7

Ali: Nice to meet you, _____.

8

Alicia: Well, _____ come _____ and have a _____.

9 .... 10 11

Beth, Ali: _____!

12

Now read the conversation with a group of three. Practice stressing words.

Reductions

Strategy

Understanding Reductions

When speaking, English speakers do not say some words clearly—they use a reduced form or **reduction**. We do not usually use reductions in writing.

Long Form	Reduced Form
I **don't know**.	I **dunno***.
Do you **want to** look online?	Do you **wanna*** look online?

*Note that the reduced forms are not correct written forms of words.

11 **Comparing Long and Reduced Forms** Listen to the following sentences from the conversation. They contain reduced forms. Repeat the sentences after the speaker. Note that the reduced forms (*) are not correct written forms of words.

Long Form

1. How are you doing?
2. It's nice to meet you.
3. We are going to go shopping.
4. Do you want to come?
5. You don't have to look for parking.

Reduced Form

How're* you doing?
It's nice to meetchya*.
We're gonna* go shopping.
Do ya* wanna* come?
You don't hafta* look for parking.

12 **Listening for Reductions** Listen and circle the letter of the sentence that you hear. Note that the reduced forms (*) are not correct written forms of words.

1. a. It's nice to meet you.
2. a. Aren't you coming?
3. a. I'm spending too much money.
4. a. Do you want to go shopping?
5. a. Do you have to study today?

   b. It's nice to meetchya.*
   b. Arencha* comin'?
   b. I'm spendin'* too much money.
   b. Do you wanna* go shopping?
   b. Do you hafta* study today?

Using the Internet

Evaluating Search Results

When you do a search on the Internet, you often get a long list of websites. You don't have time to look at every one. How can you decide if a site is useful? You can tell a lot about a site from its URL, or its "address."

Many URLs end in *.com, .edu,* or *.org.* The ending *.com* is often for businesses—they want to sell something. The ending *.org* is for an organization like a charity or a political group—they usually aren't selling something, but they might have information about their activities. The ending *.edu* is almost always a school or university—they often have free educational information. Here are some examples:

- www.eslbooks.com: You might be able to buy something online at this site.
- www.ohio.edu: You might get free information about a university. You might get information about work that people at the university are doing.
- www.volunteermatch.org: You might get free information about a group's activities. There might also be something to buy.

13 Practicing Your Search Skills

1. Open a search engine. Use keywords to search for a school near you that teaches English.

2. Look at the URLs on the first page of your results. Do the URLs end in .com, .edu, or .org? Print your search results page.

3. Pick one or two URLs that you think are useful. Visit the websites. Were you right? Visit one or two URLs that you *don't* think are useful. Were you right?

4. Circle the useful URLs. Bring the page to class to compare and discuss your experience.

Talk It Over

14 Interviewing Class Members

1. Work in groups of four. Write your teacher's name and the names of your group members in the spaces at the top of the chart.

2. Look at the example (Stacy).

   Example **You:**   What are you doing this weekend?

   Stacy: I'm going to visit my cousin.

3. Write your own question for item number 7.

4. As a class, ask your teacher the questions and write your teacher's answers on the chart.

5. Take turns asking your group members the questions. Write their answers on the chart.

Question	Name	Teacher	Name	Name	Name
	Stacy	_____	_____	_____	_____
1. What are you doing this weekend?	Visiting my cousin				
2. Do you like shopping at the mall? Why or why not?	Yes. It's fun.				
3. Do you shop online? Why or why not?	No. Don't have a computer				
4. Do you try to save money?	No				
5. Do you try to save energy?	Yes				
6. Do you try to save time?	Yes				
7. Your question:					

Giving Reasons

RETURNING THINGS TO A STORE

Sometimes you have to give a reason when you return things to a store. Some reasons are:

- "It doesn't fit."
- "It's not the right size."
- "It doesn't work."
- "It's too expensive."
- "I don't like the color."

When you return things:

- You usually need to bring your *receipt*.
- You sometimes get your money *refunded* (you get it returned).
- You sometimes get your item *exchanged* (you get a new item).
- You sometimes give the clerk your name and address.

```
Drawing Ink 30 ml / 95346
1 @ 1 for 10.99 MDS
                        10.99
Pencil Toppers / 13087
1 @ 1 for 2.99 MDS
                         2.99
Micro Pen .25MM B / 06363
1 @ 1 for 5.99 MDS
                         5.99
Subtotal
                        19.97
Sales Tax
                         1.59
Total
                        21.56
Cash
                        21.56
If you are not completely
satisfied with your purchase,
simply return it with your
receipt and we will gladly
issue a refund.

March 23/14:14
```

▲ A receipt

1 **Listening for Reasons** Listen to the conversation and answer this question.

What is the woman returning? Circle the number of the correct photo.

▲ Photo 1

▲ Photo 2

2 Listening for Specific Information Listen to the conversation again. Choose the best answer to each question.

1. Why is the customer returning the sweater?
- Ⓐ It's too expensive.
- Ⓑ It's not the right size.
- Ⓒ She doesn't like the color.

2. What does the customer give the clerk?
- Ⓐ money
- Ⓑ her telephone number
- Ⓒ a receipt

3. How much is the sweater?
- Ⓐ $43.99
- Ⓑ $45.99
- Ⓒ $43.95

3 Discussing Reasons Look at these two lists. On the left are items you can buy at a store. On the right are possible reasons to return the items. Match the items with the reasons. There may be more than one reason for each item.

Item		Reasons
1. shoes	_d, f, g_	**a.** It doesn't work.
2. purse	_____	**b.** It was a gift. I already have one.
3. calculator	_____	**c.** It was a gift. I don't like this music.
4. TV	_____	**d.** It's/They're too small.
5. shirt	_____	**e.** It's/They're too big.
6. radio	_____	**f.** I don't like the style.
7. CD	_____	**g.** I don't like the color.

4 Giving Reasons Practice giving reasons with a partner. Use the two lists in Activity 3.

Example

A: May I help you?

B: Yes. I'd like to return this _____.
　　　　　　　　　　　　　　　　　　　　　(item)

A: Why are you returning the _____?
　　　　　　　　　　　　　　　　　　　　　　(item)

B: Because _____.
　　　　　　　　　　　　　　　　　　　　(reason)

5 Role-Play Work with a partner. Student A is a clerk in a store. Student B is a customer. The customer is returning an item to the store.

1. The store clerk asks the customer questions and completes the Return Form below.

2. The customer chooses an item and gives a reason for returning it. You can use the list of items in Activity 3 on page 38, or you can use own ideas. (Note: You don't have to give your real address.)

Aplus Merchandise Stores, Inc. 227 Cedar Avenue, Springfield, CA, 90028

RETURN FORM

Customer's name: _____

Customer's address: _____

Items returned: _____

Reason for return: _____

Cash refunded: _____

Clerk's signature: _____

Part 3 Listening

Getting Meaning from Context

 1 Using Context Clues Beth, Alicia, and Ali are window-shopping at a large shopping mall. You will hear five conversations with Beth, Alicia, and Ali. Listen to each conversation. Write the number of the conversation next to the place. Continue to listen to check each answer.

▲ Beth, Alicia, and Ali shopping at a mall

_____ a clothing store

_____ a bookstore

_____ a sporting goods store

____1____ an ATM (automated teller machine)

_____ a bakery

Listening for Prices

Before You Listen

 2 Preparing to Listen Before you listen, discuss these questions with a partner.

▲ A pair of jeans

1. Do you ever wear blue jeans? When?

2. What kind (brand) of jeans do you like?

3. Where do you buy jeans?

4. How much do they cost?

 3 Vocabulary Preview Listen to these words and expressions. Check (✓) the words and expressions that you know.

Noun	Adjective	Expressions
❑ brand	❑ favorite	❑ a pair of (jeans)
		❑ on sale
		❑ the best deal
		❑ the lowest/best/highest price

Listen

 4 Listening for the Main Idea You are going to listen to three ads for blue jeans. As you listen, answer this question.

What kind of jeans are they? Check (✓) the correct answer.

_____ Western Wonders

_____ Wild West

_____ Wild and Wooly

5 **Listening for Store Names** Listen again. Draw a line to match the ad number to the store name.

1. Ad 1

a.

2. Ad 2

b.

3. Ad 3

c.

6 **Listening for Prices** Listen again. Draw a line to match the price of the jeans to the store.

1. $31.99   **a.**

2. $35.99   **b.**

3. $29.99   **c.**

7 **Listening to Compare Prices** Listen to the ads again. Then answer these questions with a partner.

1. Which store has the highest price for Wild West jeans?

2. Where is the best place to buy Wild West jeans? Why?

After You Listen

8 **Comparing Prices and Stores** Talk about the answers to these questions in small groups.

1. Where do you usually buy clothes?

2. Which store in your city or town has the best prices for clothes?

Listening to Online Shopping Information

Before You Listen

9 **Preparing to Listen** Before you listen, talk about the Internet with a partner.

1. What kind of websites do you like?

2. What kinds of websites do you visit or use often?

10 **Vocabulary Preview** Listen to these words and phrases. Check (✓) the ones that you know.

Nouns
- ❑ furniture
- ❑ gift
- ❑ groceries*
- ❑ online shopper
- ❑ purchase
- ❑ shipping
- ❑ transaction

Verbs
- ❑ deliver
- ❑ fill out (a form)
- ❑ place an order
- ❑ promise

_____
* This noun is always plural.

Listen

11 **Listening for the Main Idea** Now listen to the information. As you listen, answer this question.

What kind of website is SuperMall22.com?

12 **Listening to Online Shopping Information** Listen again. This time, listen for the answers to these questions.

1. In what two ways is SuperMall22.com different from other shopping websites?

First way: _____

Second way: _____

2. What kinds of things can you buy at SuperMall22.com? List three:

_____

_____

_____

3. You order something from SuperMall22.com at 1 P.M. on Tuesday. You receive it at (circle the correct time):

a. 5 P.M. on Tuesday   b. 1 P.M. on Wednesday   c. 2 P.M. on Tuesday

4. How does SuperMall22.com save time?

_____

_____

After You Listen

13 **Discussing Online Shopping** Answer these questions in small groups.

1. What are some advantages (good things) of online shopping? What are some disadvantages (bad things)?

2. Do you use shopping websites? Why or why not?

3. Will shopping online be different in the future? How?

Talking About Clothes

1 Identifying Clothing Look at the words in the box. Then look at the photos. Write the name of each item of clothing under the correct photo.

baseball cap	dress	pants	shorts
blouse	jacket	shirt	sweater
boots	jeans	shoes	sweatshirt

1. _____

2. _____

3. _____

4. _____

5. _____

6. _____

7. _____

8. _____

9. _____

10. _____

11. _____

12. _____

2 **Asking About Clothes** Look around the classroom. Ask the teacher if you don't know the name or color of any item of clothing that you see. Write the new words here.

_____

_____

_____

3 **Describing Clothes** Describe the clothes someone in class is wearing. Don't say which person you are talking about. Use color in your description. Let the class guess whom you are describing. The first person to guess correctly takes the next turn. Continue until everyone has a turn.

Example

▲ This person is wearing a blue sweater, jeans, and white shoes.

Comparing Prices

4 **Asking About Prices** Work in groups of three. Each person chooses a different letter: A, B, or C. Student A looks at the Morton's Department Store ad on this page; Student B looks at the Larson's Discount House ad on page 48; Student C looks at the Cost Club ad on page 48. Ask your partners about the prices for items at all three stores and write the prices in the spaces below. Do NOT look at your partners' ads!

1. How much are Wild West blue jeans

at Morton's? $ _____

at Larson's? $ _____

at Cost Club? $ _____

2. How much are Sun Ban sunglasses

at Morton's? $ _____

at Larson's? $ _____

at Cost Club? $ _____

3. How much are Spring Step aerobic shoes

at Morton's? $ _____

at Larson's? $ _____

at Cost Club? $ _____

Student A

Student B

Student C

 5 **Comparing Prices** Answer these questions about the three advertisements in your groups.

  1. Where is the best place to buy Wild West blue jeans? Why?

  2. Where is the best place to buy Sun Ban sunglasses? Why?

  3. Where is the best place to buy Spring Step aerobic shoes? Why?

  4. Where do you buy blue jeans, sunglasses, and aerobic shoes in your community? Why?

Self-Assessment Log

Check the words and expressions that you learned in this chapter.

Nouns	Verbs	Adjectives
❑ brand	❑ browse	❑ crowded
❑ furniture	❑ deliver	❑ favorite
❑ gift	❑ fill out (a form)	
❑ groceries	❑ look around	**Expressions**
❑ mall	❑ look for (parking)	❑ a pair of (jeans)
❑ online shopper	❑ place an order	❑ no problem
❑ purchase	❑ promise	❑ on sale
❑ shipping	❑ save money/time/energy/gas	❑ the best deal
❑ transaction	❑ spend money/time	❑ the lowest/best/highest price
	❑ try (on)	

Check the things you did in this chapter. How well can you do each one?

	Very well	Fairly well	Not very well
I can listen for the main ideas.	❑	❑	❑
I can listen for specific information.	❑	❑	❑
I can guess the meanings of words from context.	❑	❑	❑
I can identify stress and reductions.	❑	❑	❑
I can evaluate my Internet search results.	❑	❑	❑
I can give reasons for returns.	❑	❑	❑
I can listen for prices and online shopping information.	❑	❑	❑
I can use a graphic organizer to compare and contrast.	❑	❑	❑
I can talk about clothes and compare prices.	❑	❑	❑

Write about what you learned and what you did in this chapter.

In this chapter,

I learned _____

_____

I liked _____

_____

3

Friends and Family

In This Chapter

Using Language:	Starting and Ending Conversations
Listening:	Listening to Voice Mail Messages
	Listening to Descriptions of People
Speaking:	Leaving Voice Mail Messages
	Describing People

❝ The family is the country of the heart. ❞

—Giuseppe Mazzini,
Italian politician (1805–1872)

Connecting to the Topic

1 How are Beth, Lee, and Ali staying in touch with their friends and families?

2 Which way to stay in touch is the most expensive? Least expensive?

3 How do you stay in touch with friends and family?

Part 1 Conversation: Staying in Touch

Before You Listen

1 Prelistening Questions (Part 1) Ask and answer these questions with a classmate.

1. Who do you live with? With family? With friends? By yourself (alone)?
2. How do you stay in touch with (talk and/or write to) friends and family?
3. Do you like to use email? Why or why not?
4. Do you like to write letters? Why or why not?
5. Do you have a cell phone? Why or why not?
6. Do you use "instant messaging"? Why or why not?
7. Do you ever go to an Internet café? Why or why not?

2 Prelistening Questions (Part 2) Look at the picture. Beth, Lee, and Ali are at an Internet café. Talk to a group of your classmates and answer these questions.

1. How do Beth, Lee, and Ali look? Happy? Sad? Tired? Concerned (worried)?
2. What do you think Lee is doing?
3. What are Beth and Ali doing?
4. Why do you think they look like this?
5. What do you think Lee said to Beth and Ali?
6. What do you think Beth and Ali will say to Lee?

3 Vocabulary Preview

Listen to these words from Ali, Beth, and Lee's conversation. Check (✓) the ones that you know.

Noun
- ❑ phone card

Verbs
- ❑ (be/get) homesick (for)
- ❑ guess
- ❑ miss
- ❑ stay/keep in touch

Expressions
- ❑ by mail/phone/email
- ❑ What's the matter?

4 Guessing the Meanings of New Words from Context

Guess the meanings of the underlined words. Write your guess on the lines. Check your answers with a dictionary or with your teacher.

1. I see that your clothes are wet. I <u>guess</u> it's raining.

My guess: _____

2. Lee doesn't see his family often and he feels sad. I think that he's <u>homesick</u>.

My guess: _____

3. After you move, please <u>keep in touch</u> with me, so I know how you're doing.

My guess: _____

4. Beth calls her family a lot because it's not expensive for her to keep in touch <u>by phone</u>.

My guess: _____

5. Alicia uses her computer all day, so she keeps in touch with friends <u>by email</u>.

My guess: _____

6. Orlando likes to write letters. He keeps in touch with his parents <u>by mail</u>.

My guess: _____

7. I haven't seen you in a long time, and I feel sad about that. I <u>miss</u> you very much!

My guess: _____

8. I don't like to carry a lot of change, so I use a <u>phone card</u> to call from pay phones.

My guess: _____

9. Are you OK, Beth? You look sad. <u>What's the matter?</u>

My guess: _____

Listen

5 **Listening for Main Ideas** Listen to the first part of the conversation. Choose the best answer to each question.

1. Why is Lee sad?
- Ⓐ His mother's sick.
- Ⓑ His mother's homesick.
- Ⓒ He's homesick.

2. Who gets homesick?
- Ⓐ Lee sometimes does.
- Ⓑ Beth and Ali sometimes do.
- Ⓒ They all (Beth, Ali, and Lee) sometimes do.

3. Who wants to see friends and family in California soon?
- Ⓐ Ali
- Ⓑ Beth
- Ⓒ Lee

6 **Listening for Specific Information (Part 1)** Now listen to the whole conversation. Choose the best answer to each question.

1. Besides email, how often does Lee get letters from his family?
- Ⓐ one or two times a month
- Ⓑ two or three times a week
- Ⓒ two or three times a month

2. How does Beth stay in touch with her friends and family?
- Ⓐ She stays in touch by phone.
- Ⓑ She stays in touch by email.
- Ⓒ She stays in touch by mail.

3. How does Ali keep in touch with his friends and family?
- Ⓐ He keeps in touch by phone.
- Ⓑ He keeps in touch by email.
- Ⓒ He keeps in touch by mail.

4. What does Ali say about staying in touch by phone?
- Ⓐ It's inexpensive.
- Ⓑ It's expensive.
- Ⓒ It's difficult.

5. What do Beth and Ali do to help Lee?
- Ⓐ They tell him to write a letter to his parents.
- Ⓑ They tell him to call his parents.
- Ⓒ They tell him to buy a phone card.

🎧 **7 Listening for Specific Information (Part 2)** Listen to the conversation again. Choose the best answer to each question.

1. Lee says, "She's fine, but I miss her." Who is he talking about?
   - (A) his family
   - (B) his mother
   - (C) Beth

2. Why does Lee say, "Email just isn't the same"?
   - (A) He wants to talk to his family.
   - (B) Email is more expensive than a phone call.
   - (C) Email is inexpensive.

3. Who says, "Wait for me," and why?
   - (A) Lee says it because he's going to call his family.
   - (B) Ali says it because he's going to get a phone card.
   - (C) Beth says it because she wants to go to the movies.

After You Listen

8 Vocabulary Review Complete these sentences. Use words from the box.

by email	homesick	to guess
by mail	miss	to keep in touch
by phone	phone card	What's the matter?

1. Lee likes _____ with his family in Korea to hear all their news.

2. I'm _____ because I'm so far away from my family.

3. Ali, Beth, and Lee _____ their family and friends in their hometowns.

4. I don't know the answer. I'm going _____.

5. I don't have a computer, so I can't keep in touch _____.

6. I like to write and send letters in English, so I'm going to keep in touch with you _____.

7. **A:** _____ Are you okay?

   B: Yes, I'm okay, but I'm a little homesick.

8. You can use a _____ to make calls from a pay phone.

9. I like to hear my family's voices so I keep in touch _____.

Stress

9 **Listening for Stressed Words** Listen to the first part of the conversation again. Some of the stressed words are missing. Fill in the blanks with the words from the box. Some words will be used more than once.

all right	guess	matter	other	Yeah
email	homesick	miss	reading	Yes
fine	Korea	mom	sad	Why
friends	Lee	okay		

Beth: _____? Are you _____? What's the
  <u>1</u> <u>2</u>

_____?
  <u>3</u>

Ali: _____, Lee! _____ are you so
  <u>4</u> <u>5</u>

_____?
  <u>6</u>

Lee: I'm _____ an _____ from my
  <u>7</u> <u>8</u>

_____ in _____.
  <u>9</u> <u>10</u>

Beth: Is she _____?
  <u>11</u>

Lee: _____, she's _____, but I _____
  <u>12</u> <u>13</u> <u>14</u>

her, and I _____ my _____ family and
  <u>15</u> <u>16</u>

_____ in Korea. I _____ I'm _____.
  <u>17</u> <u>18</u> <u>19</u>

Now read the conversation in a group of three. Practice stressing words.

Reductions

10 **Comparing Long and Reduced Forms** Listen to the following sentences from the conversation. Repeat them after the speaker. Note that the reduced forms (*) are not correct written forms of words.

Long Form

1. Are <u>you</u> OK?

2. <u>What is the</u> matter?

3. <u>Why are</u> you so sad?

4. I miss <u>her</u>.

5. I really <u>want to</u> see my family.

Reduced Form

Are ya'* OK?

Whats'a* matter?

Why're* you so sad?

I miss 'er*.

I really wanna* see my family.

11 Listening for Reductions Listen and circle the letter of the sentence that you hear. Note that the reduced forms (*) are not correct written forms of words.

1. a. Are you OK?   b. Are ya* OK?

2. a. I don't miss them very much.   b. I don't miss 'em* very much.

3. a. I want to go to the movies with you.   b. I wanna* go to the movies with you.

4. a. What are you doing?   b. What're* you doing?

5. a. Why are you sad?   b. Why're* you sad?

Using the Internet

Limiting a Search
You often get too many results when you use an Internet search. For example, if you search for *homesickness* on www.google.com, you get over 200,000 results. Here's how you can limit your search: combine keywords. For example, combine *homesickness* and *cures* (things to help make it better). This way, you will get fewer and more accurate results.

12 Practice Limiting a Search Look on the Internet for information on homesickness. Try using the word *homesickness* with the keywords below.

- cures
- college students
- international students
- books
- counseling

Answer these questions when you do your search.

1. Is homesickness real? If yes, who gets homesick?

2. Are there cures for homesickness? If yes, what are they?

Compare your results with your classmates. Answer these questions as a class.

1. What keywords did you use?

2. Did you combine keywords?

3. How many results did you get with different keywords?

4. Did you get both *.com* and *.edu* URLs?

5. Which sites were useful?

6. What did you learn about homesickness?

13 Discussing Keeping in Touch Do you have any friends or family who live far away? How do you keep in touch with them?

1. Work in groups of four. Write your teacher's name and the names of your group members in the spaces at the top of the chart below.

2. Look at the example (Stacy).

Examples

A: Do you have friends who live far away?

B: Yes.

A: Who?

B: My friend Susie.

3. As a class, practice asking your teacher the questions and write your teacher's answers on the chart.

4. Take turns asking your group members the questions. Then, write their answers on the chart.

Questions	Name	Teacher	Name	Name	Name
	Stacy	_____	_____	_____	_____
1. Do you have friends or family who live far away?	Yes				
2. Who?	My friend Susie				
3. Do you keep in touch?	Yes				
4. Do you talk to _____ on the phone?	No, it's too expensive.				
5. Do you email _____?	Almost every day				
6. Do you write letters to _____?	No, never				

Starting and Ending Conversations

STARTING CONVERSATIONS

People often start conversations with people they don't know. Sometimes this happens at a party or in a new class because you want to meet someone new. Sometimes this happens on the street because you need help or directions. Here are some expressions people use to start conversations:

- Excuse me. I don't think we've met. My name is _____.
- Hello. My name is _____.
- Hi. I'm _____. How's it going?
- Hello. How are you?
- Hey! How are you doing?
- Excuse me. May I ask you a question?

 1 Expressions for Starting Conversations Work in small groups. Write the expressions for starting conversations from above in the correct boxes in the chart below. Some expressions may fit in more than one box. Then add your own expressions to each box.

	People You Know	People You Don't Know
Formal		Hello. My name is _____.
Informal		Hello. My name is _____.

2 **Listening for Conversation Starters** Listen to the conversation and answer this question.

Where are the speakers? Circle the number of the correct photo.

▲ Photo 1

▲ Photo 2

 3 **Listening for Details** Listen to the conversation again. Choose the best answer to each question.

1. Where is Susan from?
- (A) Seoul
- (B) Korea
- (C) Chicago

2. Whom or what does Juan miss?
- (A) school
- (B) Susan
- (C) his family

3. What does Juan hope to do in the future?
- (A) meet Susan's family
- (B) see Susan again
- (C) go to another country

ENDING CONVERSATIONS

Here are some expressions that end conversations:

- Would you excuse me please? I'm late for a meeting.
- I've got to go now. I'll talk to you later.
- It was nice to meet you.
- Thank you for your help. Good-bye.
- Let's get together sometime. Call me when you get a chance.
- I'd better get going. Nice talking to you.
- I've enjoyed talking to you. Maybe we could get together sometime.

▲ I'd better get going. Nice talking to you.

4 Expressions for Ending Conversations Work in small groups. Write the expressions for ending conversations from page 60 in the correct boxes in the chart below. Some expressions may fit in more than one box. Then add your own expressions to each box.

	People You Know	People You Don't Know
Formal	*Would you excuse me please? I'm late for a meeting.*	*Would you excuse me please? I'm late for a meeting.*
Informal		

5 Topics of Conversation Who can you talk to about sports? About your boyfriend or girlfriend? And when can you talk to them about these subjects? Work in small groups. Look at the list of people with whom you can discuss things (Who) and times you can discuss them (When) on page 62. Complete the chart on page 62 by deciding with whom and when you can discuss the following topics. Then, share your chart with the rest of the class.

Who	close friends	family
	casual (not close) friends	no one
When	at work or school	over dinner
	at a party	on the telephone

Topics	Who	When
Sports		
Politics		
Boyfriend or Girlfriend		
TV or Movies		
School or Work		

 6 Role Play People use different greetings for different situations. Read the four situations and the four possible greetings in the chart below. Then, work with a partner to write another greeting for each situation.

Situation	Greeting 1	Greeting 2
1. You see Bob every day at school or at work. You greet him for the first time today.	You say, "Hi, Bob. How's it going?" or "How are you?" (You don't shake hands.)	
2. You greet Jessica. You see her every day at school or at work, and you've already greeted and spoken to her today.	You say, "Hi, Jessica." (You don't shake hands.)	
3. You meet someone at work or at school for the first time—you've never met this person before.	You shake hands and say, "It's nice to meet you."	
4. You're in a hurry. You see Sue, a friend, on the street.	You say, "Hi, Sue." You can also say, "Sorry, I don't have time to talk." You can add, "I'll call you later.	

Role play each of the situations with a partner. After the greeting, use the expressions for starting conversations.

Getting Meaning from Context

1 Using Context Clues You will hear five conversations. Listen to each conversation and choose the best answer. Continue to listen to check each answer.

1. What is Beth homesick for?
   - (A) her family
   - (B) California
   - (C) friends

2. Who does Beth want to call her?
   - (A) Dan
   - (B) John
   - (C) no one

3. How many children are in Alicia's family?
   - (A) one
   - (B) two
   - (C) three

4. What's Ali doing?
   - (A) writing a letter
   - (B) talking on the phone
   - (C) reading a letter

5. When can Beth get the cheapest rates?
   - (A) this weekend
   - (B) in five to ten minutes
   - (C) after five o'clock today

Listening to Voice Mail Messages

Before You Listen

2 Preparing to Listen Before you listen, talk about voice mail with a partner.

1. Why do people have voice mail or answering machines?

2. What do you do when you receive voice mail?

3. Do you like to leave voice mail messages? Why or why not?

3 Vocabulary Preview Listen to these verbs. Check (✓) the verbs that you know.

Verbs

- ❑ call someone back
- ❑ come by
- ❑ expect someone
- ❑ leave a message
- ❑ look forward to something
- ❑ miss a call

Listen

4 **Listening for the Main Idea** Listen to Dan's voice mail messages and answer this question.

How many people left messages for Dan?

5 **Listening to Voice Mail** Listen again. This time, write the number of each message below the photo that matches it.

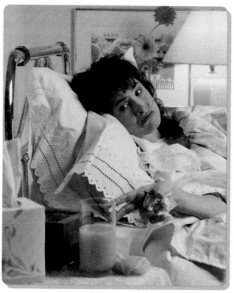

After You Listen

6 **Discussing Voice Mail** In small groups, talk about your answers to these questions.

1. Do you have voice mail? Do you have an answering machine? Why or why not?

2. Do most of your friends have voice mail or an answering machine? Describe their messages to your group.

3. Describe the best kind of outgoing message (the message that callers hear). What should you say? Should you give your name? Why or why not? Should you say that you are not home? Why or why not?

Listening to Descriptions of People

Before You Listen

7 **Preparing to Listen** Look at the photo of Ali. Describe him to a partner.

8 **Vocabulary Preview** Listen to these words and phrases. Check (✓) the ones that you know.

Verbs
❑ recognize
❑ wear glasses

Adjectives
❑ slender
❑ tall

Listen

 9 **Listening for the Main Idea** Beth is describing her friend Sue. Listen to the conversation. Which person is Beth describing? Circle the number of the correct photo.

▲ Photo 1

▲ Photo 2

 10 **Listening to Descriptions of People** Listen again. This time, listen for the answers to these questions. Choose the best answer.

1. What color is Sue's hair?

(A) blond   (B) red   (C) black

2. Which word describes Sue's height?

(A) tall   (B) short   (C) medium

3. What else do you know about Sue?

(A) She has green eyes.   (B) She wears glasses.   (C) She has short hair.

After You Listen

 11 **Discussing Appearance** How would you describe yourself on the phone to someone you have never met? Tell your partner.

▲ I'm short and thin and I have long brown hair.

Part 4 | Speaking

Leaving Voice Mail Messages

Strategy

Steps to Leaving a Voice Mail Message

Voice mail makes some people nervous. But it's easy to leave a message if you know what to say. Here are five easy steps for leaving a voice mail message.

Steps	Examples
1. Say your name and the day and time.	1. Hi. This is Lee. It's two o'clock, Tuesday May fifth.
2. Say why you are calling.	2. ■ I'm returning your call. ■ I'm calling about your ad in the newspaper. ■ I'm calling to see if you want to go to a movie tonight.
3. Leave instructions or say what you will do.	3. ■ Call me back when you get a chance. ■ I'll call you back later.
4. Leave your number. Say it slowly.	4. My number is 5-5-5-0-1-3-4.
5. Say good-bye.	5. ■ Good-bye. ■ Bye. ■ Talk to you later. ■ I hope to speak to you soon.

 1 Leaving Messages Work in small groups. Read the following situations. Choose one situation and leave a message. Record the message on a tape recorder if possible. Then listen to other students' messages. Guess which situation they chose.

1. You need to ask a question about tonight's homework. Call another student in the class and leave a message. Ask him or her to call you back.

2. You are going to a friend's apartment for dinner. You are going to be a few minutes late. Call and leave a message.

3. Your kitchen sink is leaking. Call a plumber (someone who fixes sinks) and leave a message.

4. You have a message to call Simon Majors. You don't know who Simon Majors is or what company he works for. When you call him back, you get his answering machine. Leave a message.

Describing People

2 Using Expressions for Describing People Work in small groups. Review these words and expressions that describe people. Check (✓) the ones that you know as a group.

Height	Size	Hair	Eyes	Age	Other
❏ tall	❏ large	❏ brown	❏ brown	❏ young	❏ have a mustache
❏ short	❏ small	❏ black	❏ black	❏ middle-aged	❏ have a beard
❏ medium-height	❏ slim	❏ blond	❏ blue	❏ old	❏ have bangs
	❏ thin	❏ gray	❏ green	❏ in his/her teens, twenties, thirties, etc.	❏ have freckles
	❏ heavy	❏ white	❏ gray	❏ in his/her early/middle/ late twenties, etc.	❏ have a scar
		❏ long			❏ wear glasses
		❏ short			
		❏ medium-length			
		❏ bald			

3 Describing People Work with a partner. Student A has just seen a robbery. One of the people in the following photos was the robber. Student A describes the robber to Student B. Student B is a police officer. Student B picks the robber from the photos. Then trade roles.

▲ Photo 1

▲ Photo 2

▲ Photo 3

▲ Photo 4

▲ Photo 5

Bring pictures of people from magazines or newspapers to class. Work in small groups. Mix all the pictures together. Take turns describing one of the people in a picture to your group members. The other students will try to find the picture that you describe.

Self-Assessment Log

Check the words and expressions that you learned in this chapter.

Noun
- ❑ phone card

Verbs
- ❑ (be/get) homesick (for)
- ❑ call someone back
- ❑ come by
- ❑ expect someone
- ❑ guess
- ❑ leave a message
- ❑ look forward to something
- ❑ miss
- ❑ miss a call
- ❑ recognize
- ❑ stay/keep in touch
- ❑ wear glasses

Adjectives
- ❑ slender
- ❑ tall

Expressions
- ❑ by mail/phone/email
- ❑ What's the matter?

Check the things you did in this chapter. How well can you do each one?

	Very well	Fairly well	Not very well
I can listen for the main ideas.	❑	❑	❑
I can listen for specific information.	❑	❑	❑
I can guess the meanings of words from context.	❑	❑	❑
I can listen for and understand stress and reductions.	❑	❑	❑
I can limit my Internet search results.	❑	❑	❑
I can start and end conversations.	❑	❑	❑
I can listen to and understand voice mail messages.	❑	❑	❑
I can leave voice mail messages.	❑	❑	❑
I can understand descriptions of people.	❑	❑	❑
I can describe people.	❑	❑	❑

Write about what you learned and what you did in this chapter.

In this chapter,

I learned _____

_____

I liked _____

_____

Health Care

In This Chapter

Using Language: Giving Advice

Listening: Listening to Instructions
Listening to Complaints

Speaking: Discussing Health Advice and Habits
Talking About Body Parts

❝ The first wealth is health. ❞

—Ralph Waldo Emerson,
U.S. poet and essayist (1803–1882)

1. Ali is sick. What do you think is wrong with him?

2. What kinds of sicknesses can you think of? List five with your group.

3. What should you do if you have a cold? What about the flu? List five things for each.

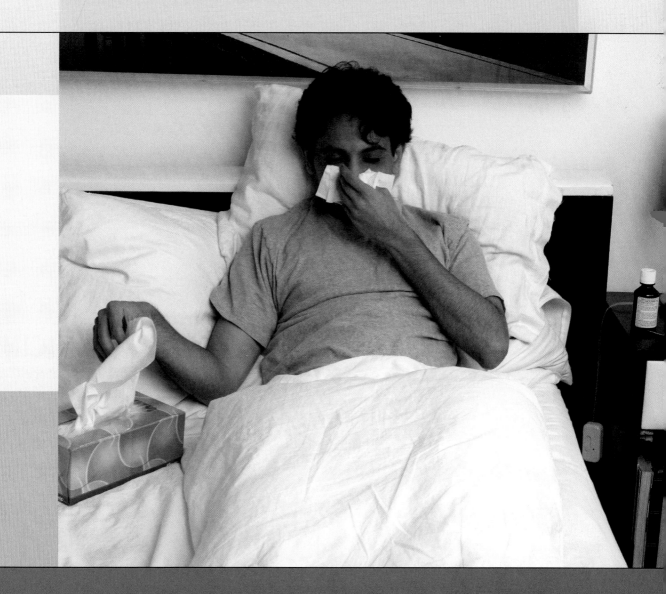

Before You Listen

1 **Prelistening Questions** Ask and answer these questions with a classmate.

1. How often do you catch a cold?

2. How often do you get the flu?

3. How often do you go to a clinic or hospital to see a doctor?

4. When did you see a doctor last (most recently)?

5. Where and why did you see the doctor?

6. Does your school have a student health clinic? If yes, describe it.

7. A hospital has many services. Describe the following services:
   a. a 24-hour pharmacy (drug store)
   b. an ER (emergency room)
   c. Family Medicine

8. What is medical insurance?

9. Why do people need medical insurance?

10. What kind of insurance do you have (e.g., car, medical, home, life)?

Look at the photos below and answer the questions on page 73 with your classmate.

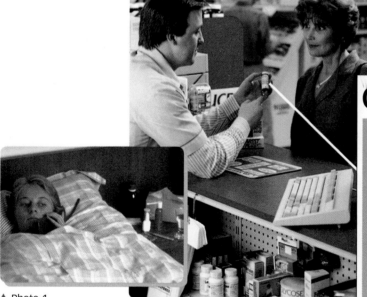

COUGH MEDICINE

Indications:
Temporarily relieves cough due to minor throat and bronchial irritation as may occur with a cold.

Directions:
Do not take more than 8 capsules in any 24-hour period.

Adults and children 12 years and over:
Take 2 capsules every 6 to 8 hours, as needed.

Children under 12 years: Ask a doctor.
Store at 68–77°F (20–25°C). Avoid excessive heat above 104°F (40°C). Protect from light.

▲ Photo 1

▲ Photo 2

1. What do you think is wrong with the woman in Photo 1?

2. Who do you think the woman in Photo 1 is calling?

3. What do you think the woman in Photo 1 will say?

4. What is the woman in Photo 2 doing?

5. Where do you think the woman in Photo 2 is?

6. What do you think the woman in Photo 2 will say?

 2 **Vocabulary Preview** Ali is calling the Faber Hospital health clinic. Listen to these words and expressions from Ali's conversation. Check (✓) the ones that you know.

Nouns
- ❑ emergency
- ❑ (the) flu
- ❑ health clinic
- ❑ ID card
- ❑ insurance card/insurance number
- ❑ menu options

Verbs
- ❑ hang up
- ❑ make an appointment
- ❑ press
- ❑ stay on the line

3 **Guessing the Meanings of New Words from Context** Guess the meanings of the underlined words. Write your guesses on the lines. Check your answers with a dictionary or with your teacher.

1. You can't walk into a doctor's office to see the doctor at any time that you want. You have to see the doctor on a specific day, so you have to <u>make an appointment</u> first.

   My guess: _____

2. The university has a <u>health clinic</u>; all the students go there when they are sick.

   My guess: _____

3. When Ali came to the university, he got an <u>ID card</u> with his name, address, photo, and student number on it.

   My guess: _____

4. Ali has a health <u>insurance card</u>. He has to bring it every time he visits the health clinic.

   My guess: _____

5. I feel sick: I'm hot and I ache all over. I think that I have <u>the flu</u>.

   My guess: _____

6. If this call is an <u>emergency</u>, please call 9-1-1. The 9-1-1 operator will help you or send someone to you quickly.

   My guess: _____

7. Please <u>stay on the line</u> and wait to talk to an operator.

   My guess: _____

8. Listen to the <u>menu options</u> before choosing a number. For the pharmacy, press 1.

My guess: _____

9. <u>Press</u> or say "zero" for the operator.

My guess: _____

10. When you finish your phone call, please don't forget to <u>hang up</u>.

My guess: _____

Listen

4 **Listening for Main Ideas (Part 1)** Listen to the first part of Ali's phone call. Choose the best answer to each question.

1. What is Ali listening to at first?
- (A) the hospital menu options
- (B) the hospital operator
- (C) the clinic doctor

2. If this were an emergency, what should Ali do?
- (A) Press "1."
- (B) Hang up and call 9-1-1.
- (C) Call the health clinic.

3. Who does Ali talk to?
- (A) someone at the pharmacy
- (B) someone in "Family Medicine"
- (C) someone at the health clinic

5 **Listening for Main Ideas (Part 2)** Now listen to the whole phone call. Choose the best answer to each question.

1. What does Ali do after he listens to the menu options?
- (A) He presses "1" for the 24-hour pharmacy.
- (B) He presses "2" for Family Medicine.
- (C) He presses "3" for the health clinic.

2. Why is Ali calling the health clinic?
- (A) He thinks he has the flu.
- (B) He wants to make an appointment to see a doctor.
- (C) both a and b

3. What should Ali bring to the appointment?
- (A) his student ID and health insurance card
- (B) some money
- (C) both a and b

Listening for Specific Information Listen to Ali's phone call again. Choose the best answer to each question.

1. When is Ali's appointment?
   - (A) this afternoon at one o'clock
   - (B) tomorrow afternoon at one o'clock
   - (C) the day after tomorrow at one o'clock

2. Ali says, "I'd like to see a doctor." What does the clinic receptionist say?
   - (A) "All right. Come in tomorrow afternoon at one o'clock."
   - (B) "All right. You should come in tomorrow afternoon at one o'clock."
   - (C) "All right. Could you come in tomorrow afternoon at one o'clock?"

3. At the end of the conversation, what else does the clinic receptionist remind Ali to bring?
   - (A) his ID card
   - (B) his health insurance card
   - (C) money

After You Listen

7 **Vocabulary Review** Complete the sentences below. Use the words from the box.

emergency	insurance card	to hang up
health clinic	menu options	to make an appointment
ID card	stay on the line	the flu

1. Ali's very sick. He may have _____ or a cold.

2. Ali wants _____ to see a doctor tomorrow.

3. Here is my _____. It shows my name and address.

4. He's sick. He's going to the _____.

5. He's going to need his health _____ when he goes to the clinic.

6. Ali doesn't need to call 9-1-1 because it's not a/an _____.

7. Listen carefully to the _____ before choosing a number.

8. No one is answering the phone; I'm going _____ and try to call again.

9. If you need to speak to the operator, press "0" or just

_____.

Stress

8 Listening for Stressed Words Listen to the first part of the conversation again. Some of the stressed words are missing. Fill in the blanks with words from the box. Some words may be used more than once.

afternoon	bring	flu	insurance	No	think
appointment	card	help	like	Oh	tomorrow
awful	doctor	ID	money	one o'clock	Would

Receptionist: Health Clinic. Can I _____ you?

　　　　　　　　　　　　　　　　　　1

Ali: Yes. I _____ I have the _____.

　　　　　　　　　　2　　　　　　　　　　　　　3

　　　I feel _____.

　　　　　　　　4

Receptionist: _____ you _____ to make an

　　　　　　　　　　5　　　　　　　　　　6

　　　_____?

　　　　　7

Ali: Yes, I'd _____ to see a _____.

　　　　　　　　　　8　　　　　　　　　　　9

Receptionist: All right. Could you come in _____

　　　　　　　　　　　　　　　　　　　　　　10

　　　_____ at _____?

　　　　　11　　　　　　　　　　12

Ali: Yes, I can come then. _____! Should I

　　　　　　　　　　　　　　13

　　　_____ any _____?

　　　　　14　　　　　　　15

Receptionist: _____—just your _____ and

　　　　　　　　16　　　　　　　　　　17

　　　_____ _____.

　　　　　18　　　　　　　19

Now read the conversation with a partner. Practice stressing words.

Reductions

9 Comparing Long and Reduced Forms Listen to the sentences from the conversation. Repeat them after the speaker. Note that the reduced forms (*) are not correct written forms of words.

Long Form	**Reduced Form**
1. Can I help you?	C'n* I help you?
2. Would you like to make an appointment?	Wudja* like to make an appointment?
3. Could you come in tomorrow afternoon at one?	Cudja* come in tomorrow afternoon at one?
4. No—just your ID and insurance card.	No—justcher* ID 'n* insurance card.

10 **Listening for Reductions** Listen and then circle the letter of the sentence that you hear. Note that the reduced forms (*) are not the correct written forms of words.

1. a. Can I help you?

   b. C'n* I help you?

2. a. Would you like to make an appointment?

   b. Wudja* like to make an appointment?

3. a. Could you come in tomorrow afternoon at one?

   b. Cudja* come in tomorrow afternoon at one?

4. a. No—just your ID and insurance card.

   b. No—justcher* ID 'n* insurance card.

Using the Internet

Pronouncing Dictionaries

You can use the Internet to find out how to pronounce words. Try using the keywords *pronouncing dictionary* or *pronunciation dictionary.* Combine these with the keyword *English* to limit your results. Remember to look at the URL. The URL can tell you if the website will be useful.

11 **Practicing Your Search Skills** Look on the Internet for an English pronouncing dictionary. Remember to combine keywords and to check the URLs. Use the pronouncing dictionary to practice pronouncing the words in the box from this chapter.

appointment	emergency	insurance
clinic	headache	thermometer

Discuss your results with the class.

1. What keyword combinations did you use?

2. Did you check the URLs before you went to each site?

3. What is the best pronouncing dictionary on the Internet?

Talk It Over

12 Discussing Solutions to Health Problems Look at the problems in the left column of the chart. Write your solution for each problem in the chart. Then, talk about what to do with your partner. Do you agree with each other? If not, why not? Write your partner's solutions in the chart.

	Solution: You	Solution: Your Partner
1. You have a bad headache.		
2. You accidentally eat or drink something bad.		
3. You are very sad and upset.		
4. You cut yourself badly.		
5. You have a bad toothache.		
6. There's a fire in your apartment.		

Giving Advice

USING MODALS TO GIVE ADVICE

Sometimes people tell you their problems and you want to give advice. To do this, you can use modals such as *could, might, should,* and *have to.* Use *have to* for a very strong suggestion. *Should* is a little less strong. Use *could* and *might* when you don't want to give strong advice.

Modal	
could	least strong
might	
should	↓
have to	strongest

Examples

Problem:	I'm homesick.
Advice:	You **could** call your family.
	You **should** call your family.
	You **have to** call your family!

Before You Listen

1 Vocabulary Preview Rick is giving Ramona advice. Listen to these words and expressions from their conversation. Check (✓) the ones that you know.

Nouns
❑ argument
❑ friends

Adjective
❑ angry

▲ "What should I do?"

Listen

2 **Listening for Main Ideas** Listen to the conversation and answer these questions with a partner.

1. What is Ramona's problem?

2. What is Rick's advice?

3 **Listening for Specific Information** Listen to the conversation again. Choose the best answer to each question.

1. What happened to Ramona?
   - (A) She had an argument with Sue.
   - (B) She has a new friend named Sue.
   - (C) She had a party with Sue.

2. What does Rick say Sue probably feels?
   - (A) She's happy.
   - (B) She's sad.
   - (C) She's angry.

3. What advice does Rick give?
   - (A) Call Sue first, then send a letter.
   - (B) Send Sue a letter, and then call.
   - (C) Call Sue and send a letter today.

After You Listen

4 **Giving Advice** With a partner, take turns giving advice. The student who has a problem can choose from the list of problems or make up his or her own. The student who gives advice can use the advice expressions.

Problems

My neighbors are noisy. I can't sleep.

I miss my family and friends at home.

I'm afraid to speak English outside of class.

My roommate/boyfriend/girlfriend watches TV all the time.

I never have enough money.

Advice Expressions

You should _____

You could _____

You might _____

You have to _____

You don't have to _____

5 Role Play With a partner, role play one of the problems from Activity 4 for the class. Then, listen to other students' role plays and answer the questions in the chart.

Questions	Role Play 1	Role Play 2	Role Play 3
1. What was the problem?			
2. What was the advice?			
3. Do you agree with the advice?			
4. If you don't agree, what advice would you give?			

Part 3 Listening

Getting Meaning from Context

 1 Vocabulary Preview You are going to hear some telephone calls. Listen to these words and expressions from the telephone calls. Check (✓) the ones that you know.

Nouns
- ❏ cavity
- ❏ (dental) cleaning
- ❏ checkup
- ❏ (eye) exam

Verb
- ❏ take your temperature

Adjective
- ❏ stolen

▲ "I've got a really bad headache."

2 Using Context Clues Here is a list of services that you can call when you need help. Read the list of services in the box and make sure that you understand each one.

the dental clinic	the fire department	the police department
the eye clinic	the health clinic	

1. You will hear five telephone calls. The first part of each call is missing.

2. Listen to the question for each call: Who is the speaker calling? Write the number of each call in the blanks below.

_____ the health clinic   _____ the police department

_____ the dental clinic   _____ the eye clinic

_____ the fire department

3. Continue to listen to check your answer.

 Listening to Instructions

Before You Listen

 3 Preparing to Listen Before you listen, talk about illnesses with a partner.

1. Do you ever get sick?

2. What do you do when you are sick?

▲ Listening to instructions at a clinic

 4 Vocabulary Preview You are going to hear a conversation at a health clinic. Listen to these words from the conversation. Check (✓) the ones that you know.

Nouns
- ❏ aspirin
- ❏ (a) cold
- ❏ drugstore
- ❏ fever
- ❏ flu
- ❏ fluids
- ❏ medicine
- ❏ prescription

Verbs
- ❏ ache
- ❏ cough
- ❏ sneeze

Listen

 5 Listening for the Main Idea Ali is at the health clinic. Listen to the conversation and answer this question.

What's wrong with Ali?

6 **Listening to Instructions** Listen again. This time, look at each photo. Listen to the doctor's advice. Cross out the incorrect words in the sentence next to each photo.

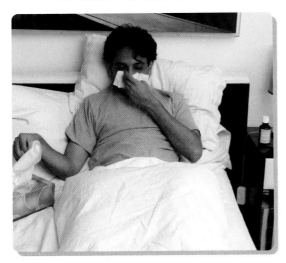

1. You should (go to school/stay in bed) and (exercise/rest) as much as possible.

2. You can take (two aspirin/four aspirin) (four times/two times) a day. That will help the fever and the aches and pains.

3. Be sure to (drink plenty of fluids/eat plenty of fruits). Fruit juice and (coffee/hot tea) are the best.

4. Here's a prescription for some (cold/cough) medicine. You can take it to any (department store/drugstore).

5. Be sure to take your medicine (when you feel bad/with your meals) because it might (upset your stomach/upset your mother).

Listen again and check your answers.

After You Listen

 7 Discussing Your Opinion Discuss your answers to these questions in small groups.

1. Talk about home remedies (things that you make at home to make you feel better). Do you use any home remedies when you get sick?

2. In your opinion, do herbal remedies (remedies that come from plants) work very well for colds and the flu? Which ones work? How do they help?

Listening to Complaints

Before You Listen

8 Preparing to Listen You are going to hear several people explain different complaints. Before you listen, discuss this question with a classmate.

What illnesses and other problems can cause pain?

9 Vocabulary Preview Listen to these words and phrases. Check (✓) the ones that you know.

Nouns	Verbs	Expression
❑ ankle	❑ break (a leg)	❑ (an illness) is going around
❑ bandage	❑ sprain (an ankle)	
❑ headache	❑ vomit	

Listen

10 Listening for Main Ideas Listen to the complaints and answer these questions.

1. How many speakers do we hear? _____

2. How many speakers say that they are in pain? _____

3. What kind of pain do they have? _____

_____

_____

11 Listening for Specific Information Listen again. This time, choose one of the following statements as advice for each speaker. Write the number of the speaker next to the best advice for that speaker's complaint.

_____ You should take two aspirin for the pain and see a dentist as soon as possible.

_____ You should wrap a tight bandage around your ankle. Don't walk on it for a few days.

_____ You can take some medicine from the drugstore for the sneezing and coughing. Drink plenty of fluids and try to rest.

_____ You should take two aspirin. See a doctor if your head still hurts tomorrow.

_____ You should go to a doctor and get an X-ray.

_____ You shouldn't eat anything for two or three hours—until you stop vomiting. Then you can have clear fluids. If that doesn't work, see a doctor.

After You Listen

12 Discussing Complaints Discuss the complaints in Activity 11 with a partner. Compare your answers. Did you both choose the same advice for each complaint? What are some other remedies for each complaint?

Part 4 | Speaking

Discussing Health Advice and Habits

1 Discussing Health Advice Work in small groups. Answer these questions.

1. What do you do when you have a cold?
2. What special foods do you eat? What special drinks do you have?
3. What advice does your mother give you?

Share your answers with the class. Do the other students do different things when they have colds? What is the best advice?

2 Role-Play With a partner, role-play a conversation between a patient and a doctor. Student A is the patient; Student B is the doctor. The patient has a cold or the flu; the doctor gives advice. Then change roles.

3 Asking About Health Habits How healthy are the students in your class? You are going to do a health survey to find out. Work in small groups. Ask the students in your group the questions in the chart. For Questions 1 through 5, put a check (✓) in the chart for each *Yes* or *No* answer. For Question 6, write the answers on the lines. Don't write down the students' names.

Questions	Yes	No
1. Do you exercise or play a sport?		
2. Are you at the right weight?		
3. Do you smoke?		
4. Do you get at least eight hours of sleep every night?		
5. Do you eat fruits and vegetables every day?		
6. What is your biggest health worry? _____		

As a class, talk about the answers to the questions. Is your class healthy?

Talking About Body Parts

4 Identifying Body Parts Work with a partner to identify these parts of the body on the photo of Lee below.

ankle	elbow	head	shoulder
arm	eyes	knee	stomach
back	finger	leg	thigh
cheeks	foot (feet)	neck	toe
chest	forehead	nose	waist
chin	hair	shin	wrist
ear	hand		

This is Lee's forehead.

These are Lee's feet.

5 **Teaching an Exercise** Think of an exercise to teach the class. Tell the class how to do your exercise. The class follows your instructions and does each exercise.

Example

> Stand up straight.
>
> Hold your hands up over your head.
>
> Bend over and touch your toes with your fingers; bend your knees a little.
>
> Repeat ten times.

▲ Bend over and touch your toes with your fingers.

6 **Discussing Exercise** Do people exercise more or less than they did 30 years ago? Work in small groups. Fill in the chart below with the things people did for exercise 30 years ago and with the things they do now.

	Today	30 Years Ago
1. What do/did people do for exercise?		
2. Are/Were people interested in exercise?		
3. What sports do/did people play?		
4. What sports do/did people watch?		

Self-Assessment Log

Check the words and expressions that you learned in this chapter.

Nouns
- ❏ ankle
- ❏ argument
- ❏ aspirin
- ❏ bandage
- ❏ cavity
- ❏ checkup
- ❏ (a) cold
- ❏ (dental) cleaning
- ❏ drugstore
- ❏ emergency
- ❏ (eye) exam
- ❏ fever
- ❏ flu
- ❏ fluids
- ❏ friends
- ❏ headache
- ❏ health clinic
- ❏ ID card
- ❏ insurance card/ insurance number
- ❏ medicine
- ❏ menu options
- ❏ prescription

Verb
- ❏ ache
- ❏ break (a leg)
- ❏ cough
- ❏ hang up
- ❏ make an appointment
- ❏ press
- ❏ sneeze
- ❏ sprain (an ankle)
- ❏ stay on the line
- ❏ take your temperature
- ❏ vomit

Adjectives
- ❏ angry
- ❏ stolen

Expression
- ❏ (an illness) is going around

Check the things you did in this chapter. How well can you do each one?

	Very well	Fairly well	Not very well
I can listen for the main ideas.	❏	❏	❏
I can listen for specific information.	❏	❏	❏
I can guess the meanings of words from context.	❏	❏	❏
I can identify and use stress and reductions.	❏	❏	❏
I can understand health complaints and doctor's instructions.	❏	❏	❏
I can give advice using modals.	❏	❏	❏
I can search for pronouncing dictionaries on the Internet.	❏	❏	❏
I can talk about health and habits.	❏	❏	❏

Write about what you learned and what you did in this chapter.

In this chapter,

I learned _____

_____

I liked _____

_____

5

Men and Women

In This Chapter

Using Language: Making Small Talk

Listening: Listening to Invitations
Listening to Responses

Speaking: Invitations and Celebrations

❝ Men need women more than women need men. ❞

—Elizabeth Gould Davis,
U.S. librarian and writer (1910–1974)

Connecting to the Topic

1. Describe the people in the photo. Do you think that they are friends?

2. Is it easy for men and women to be friends? Why or why not?

3. What do you like to do with your female friends? What do you like to do with your male friends?

Before You Listen

 1 **Previewing the Topic** Look at the photos. Talk to a classmate and answer the questions on page 93.

▲ Photo 1

▲ Photo 2

▲ Photo 3

1. Why do you think Beth is on the phone in Photo 1?

2. What do you think Alicia is asking Beth in Photo 2?

3. What do you think Beth is saying in Photo 2?

4. What do you think Lee is talking about in Photo 3?

5. How do Beth and Alicia look (happy, surprised interested) in Photo 3? Why?

2 **Vocabulary Preview** Alicia and Lee are at Beth's apartment. Listen to these words from their conversation. Check (✓)the words that you know.

Nouns	Verbs	Expression
❏ matchmaker	❏ ask (someone) out	❏ on a date
❏ permission	❏ date/make a date (with someone)	
	❏ go out (with someone)	

3 **Guessing the Meanings of New Words from Context** Guess the meanings of the underlined words. Write your guesses on the lines. Check your answers with a dictionary or with your teacher.

1. David is going to <u>ask</u> Jennifer <u>out</u>. He's calling her right now to ask her to go to the movies.

   My guess: _____

2. Many children need <u>permission</u> before they can take snacks from the refrigerator. Other parents, however, let children have snacks whenever they want.

   My guess: _____

3. Beth and a guy she likes, Michel, are going <u>on a date</u> tomorrow night. They'll have dinner and then go to a movie together.

   My guess: _____

4. Some cultures have <u>matchmakers</u> to help people find someone to marry.

   My guess: _____

5. I only <u>go out with</u> guys who have a good sense of humor. I like to have fun on my dates.

   My guess: _____

4 **Listening for Main Ideas (Part 1)** Listen to the first part of the conversation. Choose the best answer to each question.

1. Why did Michel call Beth?
- Ⓐ He asked Beth to meet him after their computer class.
- Ⓑ He's Beth's boyfriend.
- Ⓒ He wanted to ask Beth out.

2. What does Alicia think?
- Ⓐ She's a little surprised that Beth has a date.
- Ⓑ She thinks it's nice that Beth has a date.
- Ⓒ both a and b

5 **Listening for Main Ideas (Part 2)** Now listen to the whole conversation. Choose the best answer to each question.

1. What does Lee say about his friend Varun?
- Ⓐ He's from India.
- Ⓑ He needs his parent's permission to go out on a date.
- Ⓒ He's a friend in his math class.

2. Who is Parveena?
- Ⓐ Varun's girlfriend
- Ⓑ one of Lee's friends at college
- Ⓒ a girlfriend of Alicia's

3. What is Lee going to do?
- Ⓐ ask Alicia to call Parveena
- Ⓑ ask Parveena if she would like to meet Varun
- Ⓒ ask Varun if he would like to meet Parveena

6 **Listening for Specific Information** Listen to the conversation again. Choose the best answer to each question.

1. What does Beth say about Michel?
- Ⓐ He's a really nice guy, and he asked her out.
- Ⓑ He's in her classes, and he's her boyfriend.
- Ⓒ He's a friend, but he will probably never be her boyfriend.

2. Why is Alicia surprised about Beth's phone call?

    Ⓐ She's sure Beth has a boyfriend now.

    Ⓑ Beth doesn't need her parents' permission to go out.

    Ⓒ Beth and Michel are strangers (never met before).

3. Why does Beth say, "That's a great idea!"

    Ⓐ because she wants Parveena to meet Lee

    Ⓑ because she wants Parveena to meet Varun

    Ⓒ because she wants Alicia to call Varun

After You Listen

7 **Vocabulary Review** Complete the sentences below. Use the words from the box.

go out with	matchmaker	permission
make a date	on a date	

1. Alicia can't go out with a boy unless she has her parents' _____.

2. Alicia is like a _____ because she is trying to find a girlfriend for Varun.

3. Beth is going to _____ Michel tomorrow night.

4. Jim called Yolanda to _____ for Friday night.

5. Jim and Yolanda are planning to go _____ this Friday night.

▲ Beth and Michel are out on a date.

Stress

8 **Listening for Stressed Words** Listen to the first part of the conversation again. Some of the stressed words are missing. Fill in the blanks with words from the box. Some words may be used more than once.

accepted	boyfriend	one	seven o'clock	tomorrow
asked	date	out	special	yet
boy	Michel	parents'	that	

Beth: OK, great! I'll see you _____ at
1

_____. Right. Bye!
2

Alicia: Hmm. Who was _____?
3

Lee: Yeah! Someone _____?
4

Beth: That was _____, a really nice guy in my computer science
5

class. He _____ me _____. I
6   7

_____, so . . .
8

Alicia: So, _____ phone call, and now you have a
9

_____!
10

Beth: Oh, c'mon, Alicia. He's not my _____—_____!
11   12

Alicia: Well, it sounds nice. I need my _____ permission to go
13

out on a _____ with a _____.
14   15

Now read the conversation with a group of three. Practice stressing words.

Reductions

REDUCTIONS WITH *DID YOU*

The words *did you* reduce to /ja/ after *What, Where, When, Who, Why,* and *How.*

Long Form	**Reduced Form**
Who <u>did you</u> see?	Who <u>ja*</u> see?

*Note that the reduced forms (*) are not correct written forms of words.

9 **Comparing Long and Reduced Forms** Listen to these sentences. Note that the reduced forms (*) are not correct written forms of words.

Long Form	Reduced Form
1. Where did you go last night?	Where ja* go last night?
2. Who did you go with?	Who ja* go with?
3. What did you see at the movies?	What ja* see at the movies?
4. How did you get there?	How ja* get there?
5. When did you get home?	When ja* get home?
6. Why did you pick that movie?	Why ja* pick that movie?

10 **Listening for Reductions** Listen and then circle the letter of the sentence that you hear. Note that the reduced forms (*) are not correct written forms of words.

1. a. What did you do last weekend?
   b. What ja* do last weekend?

2. a. Where did you go on Sunday?
   b. Where ja* go on Sunday?

3. a. When did you get up this morning?
   b. When ja* get up this morning?

4. a. How did you get to school?
   b. How ja* get to school?

5. a. Who did you come to school with?
   b. Who ja* come to school with?

6. a. Why did you take the bus?
   b. Why ja* take the bus?

Using the Internet

Review: Combining Internet Search Skills

So far in this book, you have practiced using keywords related to your topic, combining keywords, and evaluating URLs. You can combine these three skills in order to limit your results and to find the most useful sites. Note that you don't have to use little words like *in* or *the* when you do an Internet search.

11 **Practicing Your Internet Search Skills** Use your Internet search skills to find information on things to do on a date or with a group of friends in your area. First, brainstorm for names of activities or types of places to go. Then make lists of keyword combinations with your city or town's name. Discuss your results with your class.

Examples

- ice skating [your city or town]
- Thai restaurants [your city or town]
- jazz concerts [your city or town]

Talk It Over

12 Discussing Dating What do your classmates think about dating etiquette (rules of behavior)?

1. Work in groups of four. Write the names of your group members in the spaces at the top of the chart.

2. Ask your group members the questions about dating etiquette. Check *Yes* or *No* for each question on the chart.

3. Discuss your answers.

Question	Name _____	Name _____	Name _____	Name _____
1. Is it OK for someone to ask for a date?	❏ Yes ❏ No	❏ Yes ❏ No	❏ Yes ❏ No	❏ Yes ❏ No
2. Is it OK to ask someone for a date if you haven't been formally introduced to that person?	❏ Yes ❏ No	❏ Yes ❏ No	❏ Yes ❏ No	❏ Yes ❏ No
3. Should you ask someone for a date at least three days before you want to go out?	❏ Yes ❏ No	❏ Yes ❏ No	❏ Yes ❏ No	❏ Yes ❏ No
4. Is it OK for a woman to ask a man out for a date?	❏ Yes ❏ No	❏ Yes ❏ No	❏ Yes ❏ No	❏ Yes ❏ No
5. Is it OK for the woman to pay for the date?	❏ Yes ❏ No	❏ Yes ❏ No	❏ Yes ❏ No	❏ Yes ❏ No
6. If you go to a restaurant on a date and the other person is paying, should you order something cheap from the menu?	❏ Yes ❏ No	❏ Yes ❏ No	❏ Yes ❏ No	❏ Yes ❏ No
7. After a first date, is it OK to tell the person that you'd like to see him or her again even if it's not the truth?	❏ Yes ❏ No	❏ Yes ❏ No	❏ Yes ❏ No	❏ Yes ❏ No

Making Small Talk

TOPICS AND PLACES FOR SMALL TALK

People often start conversations both with people that they know and with people that they don't know. Sometimes this happens at a party, in class, or on the street. One way to do this is to make "small talk." Small talk is conversation about everyday topics such as the weather or sports.

These are good topics for small talk:

- the weather
- sports
- movies, TV, books, and music
- hobbies and interests
- food and restaurants

These are some places that people make small talk:

- waiting in line
- waiting for a bus
- between classes
- on breaks
- in school or company cafeterias

Before You Listen

1 Vocabulary Preview You are going to hear a conversation consisting of small talk. Listen to these words and expressions from the conversation. Check (✓) the ones that you know.

Noun	**Verb**
❏ (baseball) fan	❏ look forward to

Listen

2 Listening for Main Ideas Listen to the conversation and answer these questions.

1. Do the speakers know each other well?

2. What two small-talk topics do the speakers talk about? Circle the two topics in the box below.

food and restaurants	sports
hobbies and interests	the weather
movies, TV, books, music	

Strategy

Pattern for Small Talk

In the conversation, the speakers are following this pattern:

1. **Greeting.** First, they greet each other.

2. **Making small talk.** Then they talk about one small-talk topic.

3. **Making more small talk.** Then they talk about another small-talk topic.

4. **Leave-taking.** Finally, they go away from each other.

 3 Listening to Small Talk Listen to the conversation again. Write on the lines the correct expression from the box for each part of the conversation.

Greeting	Leave-taking	Making more small talk	Making small talk

_____

_____

_____

_____

After You Listen

Using Graphic Organizers: The Sunray
You can use a sunray graphic organizer to help you think of topics related to other topics. The topic of this sunray graphic organizer is "weather." Words related to the topic are on the lines around the topic.

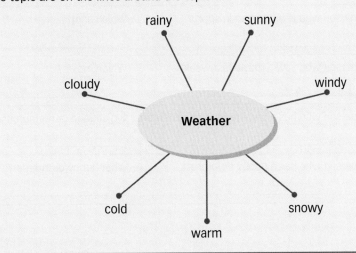

4 **Making Small Talk** Choose one of the small talk topics: sports, movies, TV, books, music, hobbies and interests, or food and restaurants. Write the topic in the center. Complete the sunray graphic organizer.

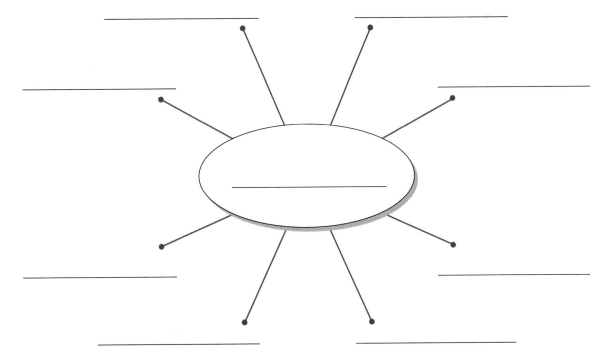

5 **Making Small Talk** Make small talk with your classmates.

1. Get up and move around the room. Start a conversation with someone in your class. Begin with a greeting. Then, make small talk about the topics you both chose in Activity 4. Finally, say some leave-taking words and move on to another person.

2. Start more conversations. Use some of the other topics. Talk to three or four people. After you finish, fill in the following chart with the information you heard.

1. Name one person who is interested in sports.	Which sports?
2. Name one person who saw a movie last week.	Which movie?
3. Name one person who has a favorite food or restaurant.	Which food or restaurant?
4. Name one person who has a hobby or interest.	What hobby or interest?

Part 3 Listening

Getting Meaning from Context

1 **Vocabulary Preview** You are going to hear some conversations. Listen to these words and expressions from the conversations. Check (✓) the ones that you know.

Nouns	**Verb**	**Adjectives**
❏ date	❏ get in	❏ modern
❏ student ticket		❏ terrible

2 **Using Context Clues** You will hear five conversations. Listen to each conversation and choose the best answer. Continue to listen to check each answer.

1. What did Beth do on her date?
   - Ⓐ She had dinner first and then saw a movie.
   - Ⓑ She went to the movies.
   - Ⓒ She saw a movie and then went to a restaurant.

2. Why is Jennifer upset?
- (A) The traffic was terrible.
- (B) Rob was late for their date.
- (C) Rob forgot their date.

3. What is Dina probably going to do?
- (A) go out with Peter on Friday night
- (B) stay home on Friday night
- (C) not go out with Peter

4. What is Pat probably going to do?
- (A) Go out with Peter on Friday night.
- (B) Go out with Peter some other night.
- (C) Not go out with Peter.

5. Why can't Anu go to the concert?
- (A) He doesn't have enough money.
- (B) He's doing something else on Saturday.
- (C) The concert is too late.

3 **Discussing Dating** Work with a partner. Discuss the answers to these questions.

1. What is a typical date for you?

2. What is your idea of a fun date?

Listening to Invitations

Before You Listen

4 **Preparing to Listen** Before you listen, talk about invitations with a partner.

1. Do you ever invite friends to your house for dinner?

2. Do you ever invite friends to your house to watch a movie?

3. Do you like indoor, sit-down dinner parties? Why or why not?

4. Do you like outdoor food parties like barbecues and picnics? Why or why not?

5 **Vocabulary Preview** Listen to these words and expressions. Check (✓) the ones that you know.

Verbs
- ❏ have someone (over) for dinner
- ❏ invite someone (over)

Adjectives
- ❏ formal
- ❏ informal

Listen

 6 **Listening for Main Ideas** Beth is inviting Michel to dinner. Listen to their conversation and answer these questions.

1. What time is Beth's dinner?
2. Is the dinner formal or informal?
3. Is Michel going to come?
4. Does Beth want Michel to bring something?

 7 **Listening for Specific Information** Listen again. This time, look at the photos. In the speech bubble for each photo, circle the words that you hear.

Hello?

Hi, Michel. This is Beth. (How/Who) are you?

Fine. How are you (doing/going)?

Great! I'm just (asking/calling) to invite you over tomorrow night. My roommate and I are having a few people (for/over for) dinner. We might rent a movie. Can you (come/go)?

Compare your answers with a partner. Did you circle the same words?

After You Listen

8 Discussing Dinner Parties Talk in a small group about the answers to these questions.

1. In your community, do guests offer to bring food or drinks to a dinner party?

2. In your community, do guests bring gifts to the host of a dinner party?

3. When you go to dinner at someone's house, do you bring a gift? If yes, what do you bring?

Listening to Responses

Before You Listen

9 Preparing to Listen Talk about accepting and refusing invitations in small groups.

1. What do you say when you want to accept an invitation?

2. What do you say when you can't accept an invitation?

3. What do you say when you don't want to accept an invitation?

10 Vocabulary Preview Listen to these words and expressions. Check (✓) the ones that you know.

Verbs	Adjectives	Expression
❑ accept an invitation	❑ apologetic	❑ some other time
❑ play (a game)	❑ bored	
	❑ excited	

Listen

11 Listening for Main Ideas Dan is talking to Ali and Beth. He wants them to do something special with him. As you listen to their conversation, answer these questions.

▲ Beth

▲ Ali

▲ Dan

1. Where does Dan want to go on Friday night?

2. Who wants to go with him?

12 Listening for Specific Information Listen again and choose the best answer to each question.

1. How does Dan feel?
    (A) excited   (B) bored   (C) apologetic

2. How does Beth feel?
    (A) excited   (B) bored   (C) apologetic

3. How does Ali feel?
    (A) excited   (B) bored   (C) apologetic

After You Listen

13 Discussing Invitations Discuss the following questions in small groups.

1. How do you feel when you can't accept an invitation?

2. Do people always tell the truth when they can't accept an invitation? Why or why not? Do you always tell the truth when you can't accept an invitation?

Part 4   Speaking

Invitations and Celebrations

1 Discussing Celebrations Work in small groups. Answer the following questions.

1. Do you celebrate when a friend or relative graduates from school or college? If yes, how do you celebrate?

2. Describe the last wedding that you attended. Did you receive an invitation in the mail? If yes, what did it look like? Who invited you? When was the wedding? Where was the wedding?

3. What kind of special events have you attended recently? Which ones might you attend in the near future?

2 Vocabulary Preview Listen to these words and expressions. Check (✓) the ones that you know.

Noun	**Verbs**	**Expression**
❏ graduation party	❏ celebrate	❏ the favor of your presence
	❏ request	

3 **Reading Invitations** Read these invitations. Then answer the questions with a partner.

Help us celebrate
Sandi Woo's
graduation party!

Saturday night,
June 14th from
8 PM to midnight
at
Caesar's Club,
355 Broadway

John, Trevor & Brittany

▲ Invitation A

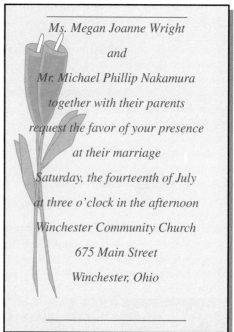

Ms. Megan Joanne Wright

and

Mr. Michael Phillip Nakamura

together with their parents

request the favor of your presence

at their marriage

Saturday, the fourteenth of July

at three o'clock in the afternoon

Winchester Community Church

675 Main Street

Winchester, Ohio

▲ Invitation B

1. Which invitation is for a wedding? Which is for a party? What kind of party?

2. Where and when is Sandi Woo's graduation party?

3. Who is making the invitation to Sandi's graduation party?

4. Who is getting married? When are they getting married? Where are they getting married?

5. Who is making the invitation to the wedding?

4 **Discussing Parties and Events** Discuss these questions. Then, on the chart below, check the parties that you go to and the events that you celebrate. Add your own ideas.

1. What types of parties do you and your friends have?

2. What kinds of events do you celebrate?

Types of Parties	Events to Celebrate
❑ Party	❑ Graduation
❑ Reception	❑ Last day of school
❑ Picnic	❑ Marriage
❑ Barbecue	❑ Birthday
_____	_____
_____	_____
_____	_____

5 **Creating Invitations** In your groups, choose a type of party or event and create an invitation. When you are finished, exchange invitations with other groups and discuss your invitations. Make sure that you include the following important information:

- for whom the party is or why it is happening
- where the party is
- when the party is
- who is making the invitation

Self-Assessment Log

Check the words and expressions that you learned in this chapter.

Nouns
- ❏ (baseball) fan
- ❏ date
- ❏ graduation party
- ❏ matchmaker
- ❏ permission
- ❏ student ticket

Verbs
- ❏ accept an invitation
- ❏ ask (someone) out
- ❏ celebrate
- ❏ date/make a date (with someone)
- ❏ get in
- ❏ go out (with someone)
- ❏ have someone (over) for dinner
- ❏ invite someone (over)
- ❏ look forward to
- ❏ play (a game)
- ❏ request

Adjectives
- ❏ apologetic
- ❏ bored
- ❏ excited
- ❏ formal
- ❏ informal
- ❏ modern
- ❏ terrible

Idioms and Expressions
- ❏ on a date
- ❏ some other time
- ❏ the favor of your presence

Check the things you did in this chapter. How well can you do each one?

	Very well	Fairly well	Not very well
I can listen for the main ideas.	❏	❏	❏
I can listen for specific information.	❏	❏	❏
I can guess the meanings of words from context.	❏	❏	❏
I can identify and use stress and reductions.	❏	❏	❏
I can understand invitations and responses.	❏	❏	❏
I can use a sunray graphic organizer to organize related topics.	❏	❏	❏
I can combine my Internet search skills.	❏	❏	❏
I can make small talk.	❏	❏	❏
I can discuss invitations and celebrations.	❏	❏	❏

Write about what you learned and what you did in this chapter.

In this chapter,

I learned _____

_____

I liked _____

_____

Sleep and Dreams

> **"** Our dreams are a second life. **"**

—Gérard de Nerval,
French poet (1808–1855)

Connecting to the Topic

1 Why do people dream?

2 How many hours do you usually sleep? Do you feel you get enough sleep?

3 What can people do if they have trouble falling asleep? List five things.

Before You Listen

1 **Previewing the Conversation** Look at the photo. Ask and answer these questions with a classmate.

1. Look at Ali in the photo. Ali is "sleep deprived." What do you think this means?

2. Why do you think Ali is sleep deprived?

3. What do you think Beth and Alicia are saying to Ali?

4. Do you think Ali studies enough? Why or why not?

5. Do you think Ali usually gets enough sleep? Why or why not?

2 Vocabulary Preview Beth and Alicia are at a café. Ali has just arrived. Listen to these words and expressions from their conversation. Check (✓) the ones that you know.

Nouns	Verbs	Adjectives	Adverb	Expression
❑ advice	❑ sleep in	❑ alert	❑ hardly	❑ can't keep
❑ chemicals	❑ take a nap	❑ complex		one's eyes
❑ research study	❑ wake up	❑ deprived		open

3 Guessing the Meanings of New Words from Context Guess the meanings of the underlined words. Write your guess on each line. Check your answers with a dictionary or with your teacher.

1. Many people worry about the chemicals in food. They think some chemicals might cause cancer or other diseases.

   My guess: _____

2. A baby needs to sleep a lot. Most babies take a nap every day.

   My guess: _____

3. It's hard to wake up in the morning. I have a loud alarm clock to wake me up.

   My guess: _____

4. In Norway the days are very short in the winter. People are deprived of sunshine. They are very happy when spring comes.

   My guess: _____

5. A simple math problem is 2 + 6 = 8. A complex math problem is $x = [y^2 \times 324y - (x + 2y)]$.

   My guess: _____

6. Oh, no! I have hardly any money—only 20 cents!

   My guess: _____

7. There is a lot of traffic in the city. Before you cross the street, be alert: Look carefully to the left and to the right and listen for cars.

   My guess: _____

8. I read a research study that says most Americans get only six hours of sleep a night. It was an interesting report.

   My guess: _____

9. My teacher suggested that I sleep more and go to parties less. I took her advice, and now I feel better!

   My guess: _____

10. I get up early every weekday, so I love to sleep in on the weekends.

    My guess: _____

11. Ali needs to study more, but he can't keep his eyes open, so he's going to get some sleep.

    My guess: _____

4 **Listening for Main Ideas (Part 1)** Listen to the first part of the conversation. Choose the best answer to each question.

1. What's wrong with Ali?
   - (A) He didn't get enough sleep last night.
   - (B) He went to a party last night and missed a big test today.
   - (C) both a and b

2. Who is worried about Ali and why?
   - (A) Beth is worried because Ali went to a party and didn't study last night.
   - (B) Alicia is worried because Ali only got four hours of sleep last night.
   - (C) Beth and Alicia are worried because Ali is not sleeping enough.

3. What does Alicia say about remembering what you study?
   - (A) It's important to sleep after you study.
   - (B) You should study in the morning.
   - (C) You should study late at night, after a party.

5 **Listening for Main Ideas (Part 2)** Now listen to the whole conversation. Choose the best answer to each question.

1. You may forget how much (what percent) of what you studied if you don't get enough sleep after you study?
   - (A) 30 percent
   - (B) 13 percent
   - (C) 70 percent

2. People who are sleep deprived _____.
   - (A) don't get enough sleep
   - (B) forget a lot
   - (C) both a and b

3. Beth says that eating foods like fish can help you _____.
   - (A) get enough sleep
   - (B) forget almost one-third of what you study
   - (C) study and stay alert

6 Listening for Specific Information Listen again. Choose the best answer to each question.

1. Where did Alicia learn about sleep deprivation?
   - (A) She read a research study.
   - (B) A professor lectured about it.
   - (C) Beth told her about it.

2. If you want to remember what you study, what should you do?
   - (A) get enough sleep
   - (B) eat more food
   - (C) both a and b

3. Why do some foods help you study?
   - (A) They have chemicals that help you stay healthy.
   - (B) They have chemicals that help you stay alert.
   - (C) They have chemicals that make you sleep deprived.

After You Listen

7 Vocabulary Review Complete these sentences. Use words from the box.

advice	deprived	to take a nap
alert	hardly	wake me up
chemical	research	

1. My grandfather gets sleepy every afternoon, so he likes

   _____ for about an hour.

2. I have a test early tomorrow. Please _____ in time for class.

3. Caffeine is the _____ in coffee that keeps you awake.

4. Away from home, I felt _____ of my family and their love.

5. Drivers should always be _____. Careless or sleepy driving causes accidents.

6. Sorry! I can't go to the movies with you; I have no time and _____ any money.

7. I read an interesting _____ study that said 33 percent of the American population has sleeping problems.

8. Can you give me some _____? I need to know how to buy a used car.

Stress

8 Listening for Stressed Words Listen to the first part of the conversation again. Some of the stressed words are missing. Fill in the blanks with words from the box. You will use some words more than once.

before	four	in	look	party	test
big	friend	it's	lot	sleep	up
can't	going	late	matter	sleepy	
eyes	hardly	library	morning	study	

Beth: Ali! What's the _____? You _____ so _____!
  1   2   3

Alicia: Yeah! Can't you wake _____ this morning?
  4

Ali: No, I _____! I can _____ keep my _____
  5   6   7

open! I was up _____ last night. My _____ had a
  8   9

_____. I only got about _____ hours of _____.
  10   11   12

Alicia: Why didn't you sleep _____ this _____?
  13   14

Ali: I have to meet my _____ group at the _____. We have
  15   16

a _____ _____ next week.
  17   18

Beth: A _____ _____? Why didn't you _____ last
  19   20   21

night instead of _____ to the _____?
  22   23

Ali: Oh, _____ OK. I studied a _____ _____ the
  24   25   26

_____.
  27

Now read the conversation in a group of three. Practice stressing words.

Pronunciation

NUMBERS

Numbers can be difficult to understand in spoken English. Different numbers in English sound very much the same. The difference between the "teens" (13, 14, 15) and the "tens" (30, 40, 50) is mostly stress: the ending -*teen* is stressed more than the ending -*ty*.

13 thir-teén	30 thír-ty	16 six-teén	60 síx-ty
14 four-teén	40 fór-ty	17 seven-teén	70 séven-ty
15 fif-teén	50 fíf-ty	18 eight-eén	80 éight-ty

9 **Pronouncing Teens and Tens** Listen and repeat these examples of teens and tens.

Teens

1. He is <u>fourteen</u> years old.
2. I bought <u>thirteen</u> new books.
3. The price is <u>seventeen</u> dollars.
4. It happened in <u>1918</u>.
5. We stayed for <u>fifteen</u> days.
6. I live at <u>16</u> New Hope Road.

Tens

He is <u>forty</u> years old.

I bought <u>thirty</u> new books.

The price is <u>seventy</u> dollars.

It happened in <u>1980</u>.

We stayed for <u>fifty</u> days.

I live at <u>60</u> New Hope Road.

 10 **Distinguishing Between Teens and Tens** Listen to the sentences. Circle the letter of the sentence that you hear.

1. a. He is <u>fourteen</u> years old.
2. a. I bought <u>thirteen</u> new books.
3. a. The price is <u>seventeen</u> dollars.
4. a. It happened in <u>1918</u>.
5. a. We stayed for <u>fifteen</u> days.
6. a. I live at <u>16</u> New Hope Road.

b. He is <u>forty</u> years old.

b. I bought <u>thirty</u> new books.

b. The price is <u>seventy</u> dollars.

b. It happened in <u>1980</u>.

b. We stayed for <u>fifty</u> days.

b. I live at <u>60</u> New Hope Road.

Using the Internet

Online Dictionaries

You can use the Internet to find out the meanings of new words. Try using the key words *online dictionary*. Combine these keywords with the keyword *English* to limit your results.

Example

| online dictionary English | **Submit** |

Remember to look at the URL (Internet address). The URL can tell you if a website is useful or not. Some dictionaries show you how to pronounce a word. If not, you can look up the word in one of the pronouncing dictionaries that you found in Chapter 4.

11 Practicing Your Search Skills Look on the Internet for an English online dictionary. Use the dictionary to find out the meanings of the following words. These words are related to the topic of sleep and dreams.

- oversleep
- nightmare
- insomnia
- [your choice] _____

Discuss your results with the class.

1. What keyword combinations did you use?

2. Did you check the URLs before you went to the site?

3. What do these words mean?

4. What is the best online dictionary on the Internet?

Talk It Over

12 Keeping a Dream Journal Write down your dreams for a week. Then share your dreams with your group.

13 Interviewing Class Members About Sleep

1. Work in groups of four. Write the names of your group members in the spaces at the top of the chart on page 119.

2. Look at the example (Stacy).

3. As a class, practice asking your teacher the questions and write his or her answers on the chart.

Example

You: Do you go to bed early or late?
Your teacher: I go to bed late.

4. Then ask your group members the questions. Write their answers on the chart.

▲ I like the morning. I'm a "morning person."

▲ I like the nighttime. I'm a "night person."

Questions	Name _Stacy_	Teacher	Name	Name	Name
1. Do you go to bed early or late?	late				
2. Do you get up early or late?	late				
3. What do you do when you can't sleep?	I read magazines.				
4. Are you a "morning person" or a "night person"?	I'm a night person.				
5. In what language do you dream?	I dream in my native language, English.				
6. What kind of dreams do you enjoy the most?	I enjoy dreams where I am flying.				
7. Do you ever have nightmares (bad dreams)?	Yes, sometimes.				
8. Do you believe dreams can tell the future?	Yes, I do.				
9. Your question:					

Agreeing and Disagreeing

▲ I don't agree. I think that . . .

EXPRESSIONS FOR AGREEING AND DISAGREEING

In conversation, we show that we agree or disagree with other people. Here are some words and expressions we use to agree and to disagree.

Agree	Disagree
Exactly.	I don't agree.
Of course!	I don't know . . .
Great!	

---

1 Identifying Expressions for Agreement and Disagreement Here are some more words and expressions we use to agree and to disagree. With a partner, decide which words and expressions are for agreement and which are for disagreement. (Circle) the words for agreement. Underline the words for disagreement.

Fabulous!	I don't think . . .	I'm not sure . . .	That's right.
Fine.	I guess so.	Perfect!	Yes, but . . .

2 Listening for Main Ideas Listen to the conversation and answer this question.

Are Lee and Alicia agreeing or disagreeing?

3 Listening for Specific Information Listen to the conversation again. Choose the best answer to each question.

1. How many hours a night does Alicia usually sleep?
   - Ⓐ eight
   - Ⓑ nine or ten
   - Ⓒ five or six

2. How many hours of sleep does Lee think is normal?
   - Ⓐ eight
   - Ⓑ nine or ten
   - Ⓒ five or six

3. How many hours a night does Lee usually sleep?
   - Ⓐ eight
   - Ⓑ nine or ten
   - Ⓒ five or six

4 Expressing Disagreement Talk with a partner. Decide if the phrases in the box below are polite or impolite. Write them in the appropriate column in the chart below. Some phrases fit in both columns.

Don't argue with me!	In my opinion . . .	That's a good point, but . . .
I don't think so.	I think it's true that . . .	That's wrong!
I'm not sure.	Let's not argue!	You can't say that.
I'm right.	Maybe that's right, but . . .	You're crazy!

Polite	Impolite

5 Agreeing and Disagreeing Work with a partner. Take turns. Say one of the sentences below. Your partner will agree or disagree with you, using expressions from pages 120 and 121.

1. Everyone needs the same amount of sleep.

2. It's good to go to sleep early and wake up early.

3. It's okay to sleep a little (two to four hours) on some nights and to sleep more (more than six hours) on other nights.

4. Adults need more sleep than children.

5. It's easy to sleep when the weather is cold.

6. When you exercise, you don't need much sleep.

7. It should be quiet and dark when you sleep.

8. Taking a nap in the afternoon every day is a good idea.

9. Men need to sleep more than women.

10. People should sleep more.

6 Disagreeing with a Friend Work with a partner. Look at the conversation below. Fill in the blanks with expressions of disagreement. There are many possible answers. Your teacher may ask you to perform your conversation for the class. The class will decide if you are disagreeing politely or impolitely!

Student A: Let's stay up all night tonight and study for the test.

Student B: _____ That's not a good idea.

Student A: _____ it is. The test is going to be really hard.

Student B: _____ if we are too tired, we won't do well on the test.

Student A: _____ If I don't study all night, I will fail the test.

Student B: _____ We can study for a few hours, then sleep.

Student A: _____

7 Role-Play Choose one of the situations in the boxes below and on page 123. Work with a partner. Plan a conversation between the two people in the situation. Decide if you will disagree politely or rudely. Your teacher may ask you to perform your conversation for the class.

Two friends are discussing where to go Saturday night. Person A wants to eat dinner, then go to the movies. Person B wants to go to the movies first, then eat dinner.

A student is discussing something with a parent (the student's mother or father). The student wants to pay a tutor to help him or her learn English faster. The parent wants the student to spend more time on other school subjects.

Two co-workers are discussing a problem at work. They need a new computer to help them do their work. One co-worker wants to complain to their supervisor. The other co-worker thinks the supervisor will be angry.

Part 3   Listening

Getting Meaning from Context

 1 Using Context Clues You will hear a lecture about sleep in five parts. Listen to each part and choose the best answer. Continue to listen to check each answer.

1. What are you listening to?
   - Ⓐ a conversation
   - Ⓑ a telephone call
   - Ⓒ a lecture in a classroom

2. What does sleep do for your brain?
   - Ⓐ It doesn't do anything.
   - Ⓑ It keeps your brain healthy.
   - Ⓒ It makes you forget things.

3. Why did Carlyle Smith teach the students a list of words and a difficult problem?
   - Ⓐ to see if they could do the problem
   - Ⓑ to teach them English
   - Ⓒ to test how much they remember

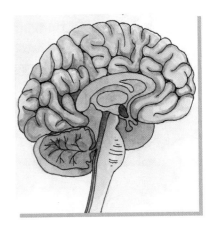

4. Why did Smith have the students sleep different amounts on the first, second, and third nights?
   - Ⓐ to see if sleeping after learning helps memory
   - Ⓑ to see if the students became angry
   - Ⓒ to make the students sick

5. How did the students who didn't sleep much on the first or third nights remember the difficult problem?
   - Ⓐ They remembered the same as the other students.
   - Ⓑ They remembered better than the students who got enough sleep.
   - Ⓒ They didn't remember the difficult problem well.

Listening to a Lecture

Before You Listen

 2 Preparing to Listen Before you listen, discuss these questions with a partner.

1. When you listen to a lecture, do you take notes? What information do you try to write down?

2. Do you review your notes before taking a test?

3. Do you try to sleep well before a test or do you stay up late studying?

Strategy

Using a Flow Chart
A graphic organizer called a *flow chart* can help you organize the steps in a process. Each step is a section of the flow chart. You will practice making a flow chart in Activity 3.

3 Thinking About Taking Notes and Passing Tests Fill in the flow chart below. What should a student do to get good grades? Start with "Arrive to the lecture on time (or 5 minutes early)" and end with "Take the test." When you finish, compare your charts with the rest of the class.

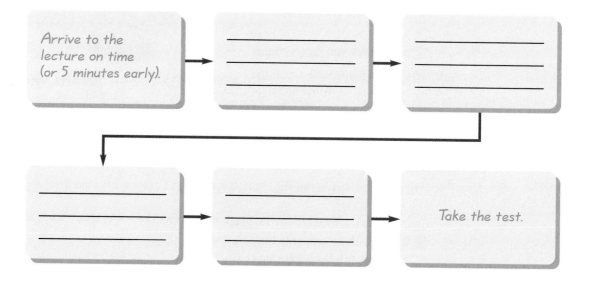

4 Vocabulary Preview Listen to these words and expressions. Check (✓) the ones that you know.

Nouns
- ❑ percent
- ❑ subject group

Verb
- ❑ solve

Adjectives
- ❑ complex
- ❑ sleep-deprived

Listen

5 Listening for Main Ideas You are going to listen to some results from the research study on sleeping. Listen and mark these statements as *T* for True or *F* for False.

1. _____ The subjects in this research study were all students.

2. _____ Being sleep deprived affected all the subjects the same way.

3. _____ The subject groups all had the same test scores.

6 Listening for Details Listen again. Fill in the chart with the information that you hear about test scores.

Subject Group	Percent Correct on the Test	
	List of Words	**Complex Problem**
Enough sleep all nights		*100%*
Sleep-deprived first night	*100%*	
Sleep-deprived second night		
Sleep-deprived third night		*70%*

After You Listen

7 Discussing the Lecture Work with a partner. Look at the sentences about the research. Mark each statement as *T* for True or *F* for False. Report to the class. Does everyone agree?

1. _____ The test on the list of words showed no differences between the groups of students.

2. _____ Students who slept enough every night answered all the questions correctly.

3. _____ Students who were sleep deprived the first night forgot the complex problem.

4. _____ Students who slept enough the first night but not the second night forgot the list of words.

5. _____ Students who slept the first night and the second night but not the third night forgot 30% of the complex problem.

6. _____ The study shows that sleeping enough is good for your memory.

8 Interviewing Classmates Find out how many hours each student in your class usually sleeps. Write the numbers below. Then report the results in percentages.

Example

There are 10 students in the class.

Three students usually sleep 7 hours at night.

You say: "Thirty percent of the students sleep 7 hours a night."

	Number of Students	Percentages
5 Hours		
6 Hours		
7 Hours		
8 Hours		
9 Hours		
10 Hours		

Listening to a Dream

Before You Listen

9 Preparing to Listen Answer the questions about dreams with a partner.

▲ A dream about being underwater

1. Do you remember your dreams?

2. Do you dream in color or black and white?

3. Do you usually have pleasant dreams or unpleasant dreams?

4. Why do you think people dream when they sleep?

10 Vocabulary Preview Listen to these words and phrases. Write the words and phrases from the box under the correct picture.

bathing suit

flippers

face mask

snorkel

_____ | _____ | _____ | _____

Listen

 11 Listening for Main Ideas Listen to Ali talking about his dream. Circle the number of the photo that shows what happens.

▲ Photo 1

▲ Photo 2

12 Listening to a Dream Listen again. Look at the following photos. Number each photo in the order of the story.

_____

_____

_____

_____

After You Listen

13 **Discussing a Dream** Discuss these questions with a partner.

1. Where did Ali go in his dream?

2. Why couldn't Ali take off his mask and flippers?

3. How did Beth try to help Ali?

4. What happened at the end of the dream?

14 **Retelling a Dream** Now retell Ali's dream by filling in the blanks.

1. Ali dreamed that he was going _____.

2. When Ali arrived at Beth's house, he was wearing _____.

3. Beth told Ali to _____.

4. Ali couldn't do what Beth wanted because he couldn't _____

_____.

5. Beth tried to help Ali _____.

6. Beth pulled on _____.

7. Ali fell _____ and broke _____.

8. Ali felt _____.

Part 4 Speaking

Telling Your Dreams

1 **Outlining a Dream** You are going to tell a small group about a dream you had. If you can't remember a dream, invent one. Start by making some notes about your dream on this page and page 130.

My dream about _____

The person/people in my dream: _____

_____

The first action: _____

_____

_____

The second action: _____

_____

The third action: _____

_____

_____

The ending: _____

_____

_____

2 **Illustrating a Dream** Draw pictures to illustrate the notes you made about your dream. Make sure you know the words to describe the objects and actions in your dream. Ask your teacher if you don't know the words you need. Write the new words on the lines below your picture.

_____

_____

_____

 3 **Telling About a Dream** In groups of four, tell your dream and listen to your group members' dreams. Answer these questions about the dreams you heard.

1. Who had the strangest dream?

2. Who had the scariest dream?

3. Who had the best dream?

4. Who had the most realistic dream?

Self-Assessment Log

Check the words and expressions that you learned in this chapter.

Nouns
- ❏ advice
- ❏ chemicals
- ❏ percent
- ❏ research study
- ❏ subject group

Verbs
- ❏ sleep in
- ❏ solve
- ❏ take a nap
- ❏ wake up

Adjectives
- ❏ alert
- ❏ complex
- ❏ deprived
- ❏ sleep-deprived

Adverb
- ❏ hardly

Expression
- ❏ can't keep one's eyes open

Check the things that you did in this chapter. How well can you do each one?

	Very well	Fairly well	Not very well
I can listen for the main ideas.	❏	❏	❏
I can listen for specific information.	❏	❏	❏
I can guess the meanings of words from context.	❏	❏	❏
I can identify stress and reductions.	❏	❏	❏
I can listen to and understand lectures.	❏	❏	❏
I can use a flow chart to organize steps in a process.	❏	❏	❏
I can use expressions for agreeing and disagreeing.	❏	❏	❏
I can use online dictionaries.	❏	❏	❏
I can talk about sleep and dreams.	❏	❏	❏

Write about what you learned and what you did in this chapter.

In this chapter,

I learned _____

_____

I liked _____

_____

Work and Lifestyles

In This Chapter

Using Language: Making a Complaint

Listening: Listening to Job Interviews
Listening to Future Plans

Speaking: Talking About the Future

❝ Choose a job you love, and you will never have to work a day in your life. ❞

—Confucius,
Chinese philosopher (circa 551–479 B.C.)

Connecting to the Topic

1 What is happening in the photo? Describe everything you see.

2 What kind of meeting is this? What are the people discussing?

3 Does this work look interesting? Why or why not?

Part 1 Conversation: Looking for a Summer Job

1 Prelistening Questions Ask and answer these questions with a small group.

1. Look at the photos below. Describe each job.

2. Which of these jobs would you like to have? Why?

3. What job(s) would you like to do in the future? Why?

▲ Financial analyst looking at a chart

▲ Architects discussing a project

2 Vocabulary Preview Ali and Alicia are at the Faber College Career Planning and Placement Center. They are at the job board looking for summer jobs. Listen to these words from their conversation. Check (✓) the words that you know.

Nouns	**Verbs**	**Adjectives**
❑ (one's) company	❑ find out	❑ full-time
❑ experience	❑ look for	❑ part-time
❑ journalism		
❑ public health		**Expression**
❑ reporter		❑ Don't mention it.

3 Guessing the Meanings of New Words from Context Guess the meanings of the underlined words. Write your guesses on the lines. Check your answers with a dictionary or with your teacher.

1. Lee worked last summer for a computer software company. He got a lot of good experience in programming and designing computer games.

   My guess: _____

2. There are many ways to find out what jobs are available. You can read the paper, look on the Internet, call local companies, or ask people you know.

   My guess: _____

3. Thousands of people in my city became sick with the flu last year. This was a public health problem, so the government and the doctors worked together to solve the problem.

   My guess: _____

4. Mina is unhappy with her current job. She will look for a job where she can work with children.

   My guess: _____

5. After the plane crash, the reporter had to interview the families of the passengers and then write a story about them for the newspaper.

   My guess: _____

6. Ali is still in school, so he doesn't have time for a full-time job. He wants a part-time job for about 20 hours a week.

   My guess (full-time): _____

   My guess (part-time): _____

7. Alicia is studying journalism. She wants to work for a newspaper or a TV news show.

   My guess: _____

8. Ali and Alicia like to do things together. They enjoy each other's company.

   My guess: _____

9. **Lee:** Thanks for helping me with my homework, Beth.

   Beth: Don't mention it!

   My guess: _____

Listen

4 Listening for Main Ideas Listen to the first part of the conversation. Choose the best answer to each question.

1. What are Alicia and Ali doing?
   - (A) They're looking for summer jobs.
   - (B) They're looking for the Placement Center.
   - (C) They're looking for jobs in Maryland.

▲ Alicia and Ali are looking for a summer job

2. What kind of jobs are Ali and Alicia looking for?
   - (A) jobs in their majors
   - (B) jobs that they have experience in
   - (C) both a and b

3. What did Ali and Alicia do last summer?
   - (A) They worked full-time.
   - (B) They worked part-time.
   - (C) They were full-time students.

5 Listening for Specific Information (Part 1) Now listen to the whole conversation. Choose the best answer to each question.

1. What kind of job does Ali want?
   - (A) part-time work in a lab
   - (B) a job in public health
   - (C) a job writing for a newspaper

2. What did Alicia do last summer?
   - (A) She worked part-time for a newspaper in Mexico City.
   - (B) She wrote international stories for *Excelsior*.
   - (C) She traveled around Mexico.

3. How did Alicia find her job last summer?
   - (A) She looked on the Internet.
   - (B) She went to Mexico City.
   - (C) She looked at the job announcement bulletin board.

6 Listening for Specific Information (Part 2) Listen again. Choose the best answer to each question.

1. Why did Ali come with Alicia to the Placement Center?
   - (A) He wants to work for the same kind of company as Alicia.
   - (B) He needs to look for a job on the Internet.
   - (C) He enjoys Alicia's company, and he also needs to find a summer job.

2. Someday in the future, what does Alicia want to do?
   - (A) She wants to write international news stories.
   - (B) She wants to write local news stories about Mexico City for *Excelsior*.
   - (C) She wants to help people around the world.

3. What does Alicia think Ali should do?
   - (A) She suggests searching on the Internet.
   - (B) She thinks he should look in Mexico City.
   - (C) She tells him to come back to the job placement board.

7 Vocabulary Review Complete the sentences. Use words from the box.

company	find out	look for	part-time
Don't mention it!	full-time	reporter	public health
experience	journalism		

1. Alicia wants to get more _____ in journalism so she can get a good job after graduating.

2. A _____ might write local news stories or international news stories.

3. Students often take _____ jobs while they are in school to earn money or get experience in their majors.

4. Alicia thinks that the Web is a good way to _____ a job because you can find jobs all over the world.

5. The website for the Centers for Disease Control and Prevention at www.cdc.gov has information on _____ problems such as malaria, tuberculosis, and flu epidemics.

6. People with careers in _____ travel a lot to get information for their news stories.

7. If you want to _____ more about jobs in journalism, you should talk to someone at your local newspaper.

8. Ali, Beth, and Lee enjoy each other's _____. They spend a lot of time together.

9. **A:** Thank you so much for helping me with my job search!

   B: _____

10. **A:** Do you have a _____ job?
    B: No, I'm a student. I work part-time.

Stress

8 Listening for Stressed Words Listen to the first part of the conversation again. Some of the words in the box below are stressed. Fill in the blanks with words from the box.

experience	job	Maryland	reporter
great	journalism	newspaper	sure
health	looking	part-time	writing
hoping	major	public	

Alicia: What kind of _____ 1 are you _____ 2 for, Ali?

Ali: I'm _____ 3 to find one in my _____ 4, public health.

Alicia: I'm _____ 5 you can. Do you have any _____ 6 in _____ 7 _____ 8 ?

Ali: Yes, I do. I worked _____ 9 in a lab in _____ 10 last summer.

Alicia: That's _____ 11. I want to find a job _____ 12 for a local _____ 13. I'd like to be a _____ 14.

Ali: Your major's _____ 15, isn't it?

Now read the conversation with a partner. Practice stressing words.

Pronunciation

PRONOUNCING MAJORS AND JOB TITLES

Many words for majors are similar to words for jobs. For example, someone who majors in *accounting* at a university might become an *accountant*. Notice that the last syllable tells if the word is a major or a job. The last syllable in words for majors and words for jobs is unstressed. It's important to listen carefully for the last syllable in words like these.

Examples

Major	Job Title
accóunting	accóuntant
jóurnalism	jóurnalist

9 **Pronouncing Majors and Job Titles** Listen and repeat the following examples of majors and job titles.

Major	Job Title
accounting	accountant
psychology	psychologist
biology	biologist
journalism	journalist
physics	physicist
technology	technologist
economics	economist

10 **Distinguishing Between Majors and Job Titles** Listen to the sentences. Circle the letter of the major or job title that you hear.

1. a. journalism
   b. journalist

2. a. economics
   b. economist

3. a. psychology
   b. psychologist

4. a. accounting
   b. accountant

5. a. biology
   b. biologist

6. a. physics
   b. physicist

7. a. technology
   b. technologist

Using the Internet

Finding Job Information on the Internet
You can use the Internet to get information about jobs. You can find out what certain jobs are like, how to prepare for these jobs, and where you can do them. For example, if you want to know more about journalism, you can try the following keywords: *journalist job description.* To find out about how to prepare for a job, try the keywords: *journalist job preparation,* or *journalist job training.* To find organizations that hire journalists, try *journalist job opening.*

11 **Practicing Your Search Skills** Choose a job title. Then look for a description of the job on the Internet. Also find training for the job and openings for the job. Discuss your results with the class.

1. What keyword combinations did you use?

2. Did you check the URLs before you went to the site?

3. What was the best site for your search?

4. What new things did you learn about the job?

12 **Working with People, Working with Things** In small groups, discuss your answers to these questions:

1. What's the best job for you?

2. Do you like working with people or with things?

Strategy

Using Graphic Organizers: Cluster Charts
You can use a cluster chart to organize groups of similar ideas. Put the main idea in the center of the cluster chart. Group related ideas around the main idea. You will work with a cluster chart in Activity 13.

13 **Filling in Cluster Charts** Look at the cluster charts below. From the list of jobs in the box, find the jobs that involve people and write those jobs in the small circles around the "People" circle. A few samples have been done for you. Then write the jobs that involve things around the "Things" circle. Add more lines and circles if you need to. Check with a partner to see if you agree. (Some jobs might involve both people and things.)

art/design	engineering	hospitality/tourism
business ✓	entertainment ✓	physics
computers ✓	health care ✓	science
education ✓		

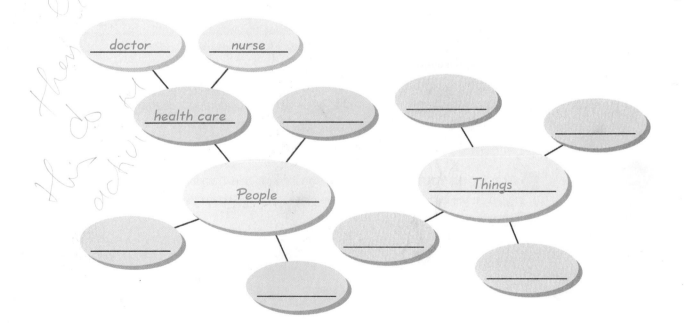

14 **What Job is Best for You?** Find out what job is best for you. Work with a partner. First, ask your partner the questions below. Write your partner's answers (*Yes* or *No*) in the spaces.

1. _____ Do you enjoy sitting at a computer for a long time, working or playing games?

2. _____ Do you like to work with other people to complete a task or to plan a project?

3. _____ Do you enjoy writing reports for school or work?

4. _____ Are you good at working with details, such as numbers?

5. _____ Do you like to solve problems by finding new ways of looking at them?

6. _____ Do you like to plan your own schedule and decide when you are going to work?

7. _____ Do you enjoy using your hands to build something?

8. _____ Do you like discussing problems with others to make a decision?

9. _____ Do you want a profession where you can help other people?

10. _____ Do you like to be in charge—to tell other people what to do?

11. _____ Do you work best by yourself?

12. _____ Are you happy doing the same things every day so you know what to expect?

13. _____ Do you like the challenge of learning to do new things frequently?

14. _____ Do you like to meet new people?

15. _____ Do you expect to work 12 to 14 hours a day?

16. _____ Are you happy when you know exactly what's expected of you?

17. _____ Are you good at persuading people to do what you want?

18. _____ Do you want to feel secure in your job?

19. _____ Do you like to travel?

Now look at the jobs in the box below. What job do you think is the best for your partner? Why? Tell the class why you think this is the best job for your partner.

accountant	politician
actor	programmer
bank teller	psychologist
civil engineer	restaurant manager
computer graphics designer	sales representative
hotel manager	secretary
medical doctor	teacher
medical researcher	travel writer for a magazine

Making a Complaint

Sometimes people have problems at work. They may need to talk to their supervisors. They may need to make a complaint about someone they work with. These activities will show ways to complain politely and professionally.

Before You Listen

1 **Vocabulary Preview** You are going to hear a conversation about a problem at work. Listen to these words and expressions. Check (✓) the ones that you know.

▲ I'm having a problem.

Nouns	Verbs
❏ client	❏ come up with
❏ presentation	❏ discuss

Listen

2 **Listening for Main Ideas** Listen to the conversation and answer these questions.

1. Who is the supervisor, Ann or Paula?

2. Why is Ann complaining to Paula?

3 **Listening for Specific Information** Listen again. Choose the best answer to each question.

1. What is Ann's problem with her job?

Ⓐ She's late, and another account manager is doing her job.

Ⓑ She doesn't like the other account manager.

Ⓒ One of the other account managers is always late, so Ann has to do her job.

2. How did Ann try to solve the problem?

Ⓐ Ann talked to the other account manager about it.

Ⓑ Ann started coming late every day.

Ⓒ Ann quit her job.

3. What does Paula suggest?

    (A) Ann should talk to the other account manager again.

    (B) Ann should stop complaining.

    (C) Both she and Ann should talk to the other account manager.

After You Listen

> ### Strategy
>
> **Making Complaints Politely and Professionally**
> When you make a complaint you should:
> - be specific about the problem
> - use positive statements
> - try not to get angry
> - try to agree on a solution to the problem

4 Making Complaints Discuss the following situations with a partner. Decide if you would make a complaint in each of these situations.

1. You bought a shirt at a local store. The first time the shirt was washed, two buttons came off.

2. You ordered food in a restaurant. It was cooked too much, and it was dry when you got it.

3. You ordered food in a restaurant. The waiter brought your food, but one of the dishes was not what you ordered.

4. At your job, your supervisor asks you to do something that is not part of your job.

5. Your neighbor is making a lot of noise, and you are trying to sleep.

6. You are at a movie theater. The person behind you keeps talking, and you can't hear the movie.

7. You get a low grade on a test. You think the test was unfair.

5 Who Do You Complain To?

1. With a partner, choose one of the situations from Activity 4. Decide who you would complain to. For example, in Situation 1, you might complain to the manager of the store. Write a conversation. One of you will make a complaint. The other will respond appropriately. Review the complaint strategies above.

2. Then perform your conversation for the class. Did each conversation meet the four goals from the strategy you learned above?

Getting Meaning from Context

1 Vocabulary Preview Listen to these words and expressions from the conversations. Check (✓) the ones that you know.

Noun	**Verb**	**Adjectives**
❑ appointment	❑ get out of	❑ rough
		❑ tired of

2 Using Context Clues You will hear five conversations. Listen to each conversation and choose the best answer. Continue to listen to check your answer.

1. Who is Alicia talking to?
   - (A) an English teacher
   - (B) a reporter
   - (C) the manager of a newspaper

2. What does Sang-mi want to do this summer?
   - (A) work in a hospital
   - (B) study
   - (C) go back to Korea

3. What is Dan thinking about doing this summer?
   - (A) studying
   - (B) going to Europe
   - (C) visiting his friend in San Francisco

4. What does Dan want to do in the fall?
   - (A) work
   - (B) travel
   - (C) study

5. Can Sang-mi work?
   - (A) No, she can't.
   - (B) Yes, but only in the summer.
   - (C) Yes, but she has to finish school first.

Listening to Job Interviews

Before You Listen

 3 Preparing to Listen Before you listen, talk about job interviews with a partner.

1. Have you ever had an interview for a job?

2. What do you think an employer wants to know about a job applicant?

 4 Vocabulary Preview Listen to these words and expressions. Check (✓) the ones that you know.

Noun
❑ résumé

Adjectives
❑ accurate
❑ challenging

❑ impressive

Listen

 5 Listening for Main Ideas Rafael is interviewing for a job. He's talking to Claudia. Listen to the interview and answer these questions.

1. Why is Rafael interested in the job?

2. What job would Rafael like to have in ten years?

▲ A job interview

 6 Listening for Specific Information Listen again. This time, choose the best answer to each question.

1. Why should Claudia give Rafael a job with the company?
   - (A) He learns quickly.
   - (B) He needs the money.
   - (C) He thinks the job sounds easy.

2. Why does Rafael need to learn things quickly?
   - (A) He doesn't know anything about computers.
   - (B) He has to go back to school if he takes the job.
   - (C) He'll have to learn a lot of new things if he takes the job.

3. What would Rafael like to do in ten years?
   - (A) be a department store clerk
   - (B) be a department manager
   - (C) be a student

After You Listen

7 Discussing Job Interviews Talk in small groups. How would you answer the following common job interview questions? Think about what the interviewer wants to know. Share your answers with the class. Which answers do you think would impress an interviewer?

1. What are your strengths?

2. What are your weaknesses?

3. What is your biggest accomplishment?

4. Why do you want this job?

▲ What are some of your weaknesses?

Listening to Future Plans

Before You Listen

8 Preparing to Listen In small groups, talk about planning for the future. Discuss your answers to the following questions.

1. What are some situations where people ask you about your plans for the future?

2. Who do you talk to about your plans for the future? Your family? Your friends? Your teachers?

9 **Vocabulary Preview** Listen to these words and expressions. Check (✓) the ones that you know.

Nouns
- ❑ construction
- ❑ expenses
- ❑ relatives
- ❑ youth hostels

Expression
- ❑ once in a lifetime

Listen

10 **Listening for the Main Idea** Dan is talking to his father about going to Europe this summer with his friend Bill. Answer this question.

What does Dan want his father to do?

▲ Dan's father

▲ Dan in his dorm room

11 **Listening to Future Plans** Listen again and choose the best answer to each question.

1. What did Dan do last summer?
   - (A) traveled in Europe
   - (B) worked for a construction company
   - (C) stayed in youth hostels

2. What does Dan have to pay for on his trip?
   - (A) a rental car, hotel rooms, and meals
   - (B) airfare, hostel rooms, and meals
   - (C) airfare and a car

3. How will Dan pay for the trip?
   - (A) use money from his part-time job
   - (B) borrow money from his friend Bill
   - (C) sell his car

4. What does Dan need from his father?
   - (A) money for his books and expenses
   - (B) French lessons
   - (C) a new car

5. Which of these is NOT a reason that Dan thinks the trip is a good idea?
   - (A) He can learn about the world.
   - (B) He can earn some money.
   - (C) He can practice his French.

After You Listen

12 **Discussing the Conversation** Discuss your answers to the following questions in small groups.

1. Do you think Dan's father will let him go to Europe with his friend?

2. What are some concerns Dan's father might have about Dan's plans?

3. What are some other reasons for going to Europe?

4. Do you think traveling is good preparation for your career? Why or why not?

Part 4   Speaking

Talking About the Future

1 **Class Survey** Do your classmates like to plan for the future? Take a survey and find out.

1. Work in groups of four. Look at the example (Stacy).

Example   **A:** What job do you want to have ten years from now?

B: I want to be a software engineer.

2. As a class, practice asking your teacher the questions and write his or her answers on the chart.

3. Take turns asking your group members the questions. Write their answers on the chart.

Question	Name Stacy	Teacher	Name	Name	Name
1. What job do you want to have ten years from now?	Software engineer				
2. Where do you want to live ten years from now?	New York City				
3. Do you want to get married? When?	Yes. In five years				
4. Do you want to have children? How many?	Yes. Two				
5. Do you have educational plans?	Degree in computer science				
6. What do you want to change about your life in the next ten years?	Wants to have a family and move to New York City				

2 Discussing the Survey Discuss the results of Activity 1 with the class. Make notes about the questions below.

1. What jobs do people in the class want to have?

2. Where do they want to live?

3. How many people want to get married?

4. How many children do people in the class want to have?

5. What are their plans for education?

3 Graphing the Results Work with your group again. Make a chart or graph showing information from the chart on page 149. Choose from the topics in the box below or write a topic of your own.

> How many children people want to have
> What field people want to work in
> When (in how many years) people want to get married
> Which part of the world people want to live in

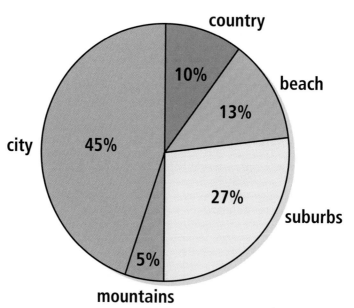

Where People in My Class Want to Live

country 10%
beach 13%
city 45%
suburbs 27%
mountains 5%

Self-Assessment Log

Check the words and expressions that you learned in this chapter.

Nouns	Verbs	Adjectives	Idioms and Expressions
❏ appointment	❏ come up with	❏ accurate	❏ Don't mention it!
❏ client	❏ discuss	❏ challenging	❏ once in a lifetime
❏ (one's) company	❏ find out	❏ full-time	
❏ construction	❏ get out of	❏ impressive	
❏ expenses	❏ look for	❏ part-time	
❏ experience		❏ rough	
❏ journalism		❏ tired of	
❏ presentation			
❏ public health			
❏ relatives			
❏ reporter			
❏ résumé			
❏ youth hostels			

Check the things that you did in this chapter. How well can you do each one?

	Very well	Fairly well	Not very well
I can listen for the main ideas.	❏	❏	❏
I can listen for specific information.	❏	❏	❏
I can guess the meanings of words from context.	❏	❏	❏
I can identify and use stress and reductions.	❏	❏	❏
I can understand conversations about jobs and the workplace.	❏	❏	❏
I can use a cluster chart to organize information.	❏	❏	❏
I can make polite complaints.	❏	❏	❏
I can use the Internet to find information about jobs.	❏	❏	❏
I can create a pie chart to graph results.	❏	❏	❏

Write about what you learned and what you did in this chapter.

In this chapter,

I learned _____

_____

I liked _____

_____

8

Food and Nutrition

In This Chapter

Using Language:	Ordering in a Restaurant
Listening:	Listening to Instructions
	Following Recipes
Speaking:	Talking About Recipes
	Talking About Nutrition

" The belly rules the mind. "

—Spanish proverb

Connecting to the Topic

1 What are these people doing? How do they know each other?

2 What kinds of foods do you see in the photo? Are these foods healthy?

3 What kinds of foods do you usually eat?

Before You Listen

1 **Prelistening Questions** Ask and answer these questions with a classmate.

1. Look at Photo 1. Where is the woman?

2. What is the woman doing?

3. What fruits and vegetables do you usually buy?

4. How do you like to buy fruits and vegetables—fresh? Canned? Frozen? Why?

5. Look at Photo 2. Do you ever eat at food courts?

▲ Photo 1: Shopping for produce

▲ Photo 2: Eating at a food court

6. These days, most big shopping malls have food courts. Why do you think they are so popular?

7. How often do you eat American "fast food" such as hamburgers and French fries?

8. Do you like fast food? Why or why not?

2 **Vocabulary Preview** Dan, Meryl, and Pat are at a food court. They are deciding where to eat and what to eat. Listen to these words and expressions from their conversation. Check (✓) the ones that you know.

Nouns
- ❑ calories
- ❑ diet
- ❑ an order of
- ❑ picnic
- ❑ vegetarian

Verbs
- ❑ decide
- ❑ order

Adjectives
- ❑ diet
- ❑ worried

Expressions
- ❑ good/bad for you
- ❑ You said it!

Guessing the Meanings of New Words from Context Guess the meanings of the underlined words. Write your guesses on the lines. Check your answers with a dictionary or with your teacher.

1. Let's make some sandwiches, go to the park, and have a <u>picnic</u>.

   My guess: _____

2. Meryl eats a lot of salads, so Pat is not <u>worried</u> about Meryl's health.

   My guess: _____

3. **Waiter:** What would you like?

   Customer: I'd like a cheeseburger and an <u>order</u> of fries.

   My guess: _____

4. He's sick because he smokes, and smoking is <u>bad for you</u>.

   My guess: _____

5. Pat doesn't eat hamburgers or other meats. She's a <u>vegetarian</u>.

   My guess: _____

6. Meryl doesn't like sugar in her food, so she will have a <u>diet</u> cola.

   My guess: _____

7. Cheeseburgers have a lot of <u>calories</u> because they have a lot of fat.

   My guess: _____

8. **Ali:** This pizza is delicious!

   Beth: <u>You said it!</u> It is really delicious!

   My guess: _____

9. Dan loves Italian food, so he can't <u>decide</u> what to order: pizza or spaghetti.

   My guess: _____

10. **Waiter:** What would you like to <u>order</u>?

    Customer: I'll have a double cheeseburger.

    My guess: _____

Listen

4 **Listening for Main Ideas** Listen to the first part of the conversation. Choose the best answer to each question.

1. What are Dan, Meryl, and Pat doing?
   - (A) They are waiting in line at a restaurant.
   - (B) They are eating at a food court.
   - (C) They are deciding what to eat.

2. Where is Dan going to eat?

    Ⓐ at a fast-food restaurant

    Ⓑ at a picnic because he likes cheeseburgers

    Ⓒ at a vegetarian restaurant

3. What do Pat and Meryl think?

    Ⓐ Dan eats too many cheeseburgers.

    Ⓑ Cheeseburgers are good for you.

    Ⓒ both a and b

 5 Listening for Specific Information (Part 1) Now listen to the whole conversation. Choose the best answer to each question.

1. Who is *not* going to order a cheeseburger and why?

    Ⓐ Pat is not going to order a cheeseburger because she's a vegetarian.

    Ⓑ Meryl is not going to order a cheeseburger because she's on a diet.

    Ⓒ both a and b

2. Who is going to have a salad?

    Ⓐ Meryl only

    Ⓑ Dan only

    Ⓒ both Meryl and Dan

3. What is bad about cola and other sodas?

    Ⓐ They have a lot of sugar.

    Ⓑ They are bad for your teeth.

    Ⓒ both a and b

 6 Listening for Specific Information (Part 2) Listen to the whole conversation again. Choose the best answer to each question.

1. At the beginning of the conversation, Pat can't decide what to have. Why not?

    Ⓐ She's a vegetarian, and there are no vegetarian choices.

    Ⓑ She's on a diet, and there are no places to order a salad.

    Ⓒ There are so many choices at the food court.

2. Why are Pat and Meryl worried about Dan?

    Ⓐ He eats a lot of fast food.

    Ⓑ He's fat.

    Ⓒ He drinks a lot of soda.

3. Who orders a diet soda and why?

    Ⓐ Pat does because she's a vegetarian.

    Ⓑ Meryl does because there's no sugar in it.

    Ⓒ Dan does because he's worried about his teeth.

7 Vocabulary Review Complete these sentences. Use words from the box.

bad for you	diet	to order
calories	order of	worried
decide	picnic	You said it!

1. Foods with a lot of sugar, like soft drinks, usually have a lot of

   _____ in them.

2. Meryl and Pat are _____ about Dan's health because he eats too many cheeseburgers.

3. Do you think _____ foods really help you lose weight?

4. We can take a long walk and eat a _____ outside on the way.

5. Doctors think that foods with a lot of fat such as red meat and ice cream, are

   _____.

6. With my tofu, I'd like a side _____ rice, please.

7. **Waiter:** What would you like _____?

   Customer: I can't _____. What's good on the menu tonight?

8. **Dan:** Look at all these places to eat! This food court is great!

   Pat: _____ It is great!

Stress

8 Listening for Stressed Words Listen to the first part of the conversation again. Some of the stressed words are missing. Fill in the blanks with words from the box. You may use some words more than once.

cheeseburger	fast	have	like	place
eat	food	healthy	order	what
fat	fries	hungry	picnic	worried

Meryl: What are you going to _____, Dan?
                                          1

Dan: I'm _____! I'm going to the _____
                        2   3

_____ _____. I want a double
        4   5

_____ and a large _____ of
        6   7

_____.
        8

Pat: Ugh! How many cheeseburgers do you _____ every week?

You had a couple at the _____ yesterday, didn't you?

Dan: Yeah . . . so _____? I _____ cheeseburgers!

Meryl: I think Pat's _____ about you.

Dan: Why? I'm _____.

Pat: But cheeseburgers have a lot of _____.

Now read the conversation with a partner. Practice stressing words.

Reductions

9 Comparing Long and Reduced Forms Listen to the sentences. Repeat them after the speaker. Note that the reduced forms (*) are not correct written forms of words.

Long Form	**Reduced Form**
1. What are you going to have?	What're* ya gonna* have?
2. I think I'm going to have some tofu and rice.	I think I'm gonna* have some tofu 'n rice.
3. We would like a couple of salads.	We'd like a coupla* salads.
4. Isn't there a lot of fat in cheeseburgers?	Isn't there a lotta* fat in cheeseburgers?
5. They don't want to eat lots of fatty food.	They don't wanna* eat lotsa* fatty food.

10 Listening for Reductions Listen and circle the letter of the sentence that you hear. Note that the reduced forms (*) are not the correct written forms of words.

1. a. What are you going to have?
  b. What're* ya* gonna* have?

2. a. I think I am going to have some tofu and rice.
  b. I think I'm gonna* have some tofu 'n rice.

3. a. We would like a couple of salads.
  b. We'd like a coupla* salads.

4. a. Isn't there a lot of fat in cheeseburgers?
  b. Isn't there a lotta* fat in cheeseburgers?

5. a. They don't want to eat lots of fatty food.
  b. They don't wanna* eat lotsa* fatty food.

Using the Internet

Finding Information About Food

You can find information about food and diets on the Internet. Combine keywords to find out things like the fat, calorie, and sugar content in foods. You can also find calorie counters on the Internet. A calorie counter will tell you how many calories are in a particular food.

Examples

| calories   apple | **Submit** |
| calorie counter | **Submit** |

You can also go to sites that have information about food and diets. Some of these are the United States Department of Agriculture (USDA) at www.mypyramid.gov, the World Health Organization (WHO) at www.who.int, or the British Broadcasting Corporation (BBC) at www.bbc.co.uk/health.

11 Practicing Your Search Skills Look on the Internet for information about food and diets. Find the following:

- a calorie counter
- how many calories a medium-sized apple has
- how many calories your favorite snack food has
- how many calories your favorite drink has
- what you can learn from one of the food information sites above (the WHO, the BBC, or the USDA)
- how many calories you should eat each day
- [your own idea]

Discuss your results with the class.

1. What keyword combinations did you use?
2. Did you check the type of URLs before you went to the site?
3. What was the best site for your searches?
4. What new things did you learn about food and diets?

Strategy

Categorizing Vocabulary Words

When you learn a new vocabulary word, it can be helpful to put that new word into a category. For example, the word *apple* goes in the category *fruit.* It can also be helpful to put words into groups. This will help you remember words and learn new words. You will practice categorizing words in Activity 12 and in another activity later in the chapter.

12 Discussing Healthy and Unhealthy Foods With a partner, talk about the items in the box below. Is each item good for you or bad for you? Write each item in the appropriate column in the chart on page 161. Then add the reason each item is good for you or bad for you. Discuss your decisions with the class.

▲ Fresh produce is good for you.

▲ Fast food is bad for you.

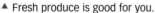

beans	fruit	salad dressing
bread	ice cream	skim (nonfat) milk
cheeseburgers	meat	soda
eggs	orange juice	tofu
French fries	rice	vegetables

Good for You	Bad for You	Reason
	French fries	They have a lot of fat.

Ordering in a Restaurant

Before You Listen

1 Vocabulary Preview You are going to hear Lee and Alicia order dinner in a restaurant. Listen to these words and expressions. Check (✓) the ones that you know.

Nouns

❑ hot tea   ❑ maître d'

❑ Italian dressing   ❑ mushroom

Verb

❑ order

Listen

2 Listening for the Main Idea Lee and Alicia are doing something special tonight. Listen to the conversations and answer the question.

Are Lee and Alicia having dinner with a group of friends?

3 Listening for Specific Information Look at the photos and listen to the conversations again. Number each photo to match the number of the conversation that you hear.

_____

_____

_____

_____

_____

4 **Ordering in a Restaurant** Now listen to the conversations again. Write the sentences that Lee and Alicia use to ask for each of the following items.

1. a table near the window _____

2. water _____

3. the mushroom ravioli _____

4. the spaghetti with tomato sauce _____

5. some lemon for the tea _____

6. the check _____

After You Listen

5 **Role Play** Work in groups of three. Two students are customers, and one student is the waiter. The customers order from the menu below. Use the words and expressions from the box. Then, perform your role play for the class.

Menu Words			
an appetizer	salad dressing	soup	salad
drink	entrée	dessert	
Customer Expressions			
I'd like . . .	Could I have . . .	I'll have . . .	Would you bring us . . .
Waiter/Waitress Expressions			
Would you like . . .		What kind of . . .	What would you like . . .

MARY'S RESTAURANT

APPETIZERS
Oysters on the Half Shell – dozen 8.95 – half dozen 5.95
Stuffed Artichoke 4.95
Nachos 4.95 – with Guacamole 5.95

ENTREES
Hamburger 5.95 – with Cheese 6.50   Chile con Carne 7.25
Grilled Chicken 8.95   Stuffed Green Peppers 9.50
Sesame Tofu 8.50   Pesto Pasta 9.50
Entrees come with baked potato or rice and vegetables.

SOUPS
Soup of the Day 2.95   French Onion Soup 2.50

DESSERTS
Cheesecake 3.50   Chocolate Cake 3.95
Pecan Pie 2.95   Ice Cream 2.50

SALADS
Spinach Salad 3.75   Small Tossed Salad 2.95
Dressings: French, Italian, Ranch

BEVERAGES
Coffee 1.25   Tea 1.25   Soft Drinks 1.25

We take Visa, MasterCard, and American Express.
5% tax added to all items
Thank you for eating at MARY'S

Getting Meaning from Context

1 **Vocabulary Preview** You are going to hear some conversations about food. Listen to these words and expressions from the conversations. Check (✓) the ones that you know.

Nouns

❑ carrot   ❑ ounce

❑ charge   ❑ produce

❑ cucumber   ❑ teaspoon

❑ onion soup

Verb

❑ beat

2 **Using Context Clues** You will hear five conversations. Listen to each conversation and choose the best answer. Continue to listen to check each answer.

1. Where are Lee and Alicia?
- Ⓐ in a restaurant
- Ⓑ in a supermarket
- Ⓒ in a cafeteria

2. What's Lee asking about?
- Ⓐ the waiter
- Ⓑ the menu
- Ⓒ the bill

3. What are Dan and Beth doing?
- Ⓐ cooking something
- Ⓑ shopping
- Ⓒ eating in a restaurant

4. Where are Ali and Alicia?
- Ⓐ at a restaurant
- Ⓑ at a produce stand (a small fruit and vegetable market)
- Ⓒ in a supermarket produce (fruit and vegetable) section

5. Which spaghetti sauce is the best price?
- Ⓐ the smaller can
- Ⓑ the eight-ounce size for $1.06
- Ⓒ the sauce for $0.99

Listening to Instructions

Before You Listen

3 Preparing to Listen Work with a partner to answer the questions.

1. When do you give someone instructions? List some possible situations. Share with the class.

2. Do you cook? What do you know how to cook?

3. What food would you like to learn how to cook? Why?

4 Vocabulary Preview Listen to these words and expressions from the conversation. Check (✓) the ones that you know.

Noun	Verbs	Adverb
❑ cheese grater	❑ brown	❑ thoroughly
	❑ chop	
	❑ grate	

Listen

5 Listening for Main Ideas Beth and Alicia are talking to Ali. Listen to their conversation and answer these questions.

1. What kind of instructions did Ali's mother send him?

2. Why did Ali ask his mother for recipes?

6 Listening to Instructions Listen again. This time, match the words on the left with the meanings on the right. Then, listen again to check your answers. Compare your answers with a partner.

1. _____ chop   a. a tool for making small, thin pieces of cheese

2. _____ mix   b. cook something in oil until it changes color

3. _____ grate   c. cut something into small pieces

4. _____ brown   d. combine two or more things together

5. _____ cheese grater   e. make thin, little pieces of cheese or other foods

After You Listen

7 **Categorizing Food** If you want to learn new recipes, you need to know the names of many different food items. How many do you know in English?

1. Work in groups of four. Each member of the group chooses one letter of the alphabet. Write one letter in each of the four boxes across the top of the following chart.

2. Write a word in each space that fits the category and starts with the letter at the top of the column. Do the first column as a class.

    For example, the letter for column 1 is *S.* For the category *Fruits,* you can write "Strawberry." Fill in as many spaces as you can in three minutes with your class.

3. Now, complete the activity with your small group. When you finish, take turns reading your answers in your group. Cross off any answers that another member in the group says. You get one point for each answer you wrote that no one else has. The person with the most points wins.

Category	S				
Fruits	Strawberry				
Vegetables					
Grains					
Meats					
Desserts					
Drinks					

Following Recipes

Before You Listen

 8 Preparing to Listen Before you listen, talk about cooking and recipes with a partner.

1. What is a recipe you know? Describe it.

2. Are TV shows about cooking popular in your country? Describe the shows. If you don't watch cooking shows, what do you think they are?

9 Vocabulary Preview Match the food words below with the photos. Write the letter of the photo on the correct line.

a.

b.

c.

d.

e.

f.

g.

1. _____ beef

2. _____ beans

3. _____ tomatoes

4. _____ onion

5. _____ oil

6. _____ chili powder

7. _____ shredded cheese

Listen

10 Listening for the Main Idea

Wally Chan has a cooking show on TV. He explains how to make easy American dishes. As you listen to Wally Chan's show, answer this question.

What food is Wally making?

▲ Wally Chan cooks

11 Ordering Steps in a Recipe Look at these photos. They show the steps for making chili, but the steps are in the wrong order. Listen to Wally's show again and number the photos from 1 to 4.

_____

_____

_____

_____

After You Listen

12 **Discussing Opinions About Food** Listen to the following statements. Decide if you agree or disagree. Write *A* for Agree or *D* for Disagree for each of the statements. Then, compare your answers with the class.

1. _____ I like onions on my hamburgers.

2. _____ Chili powder makes food too hot and spicy.

3. _____ I eat a lot of cheese—with crackers, bread, and other foods.

4. _____ Tomatoes are best in salad, with lettuce, oil, and vinegar.

5. _____ I like beans when they are cooked with onions and garlic.

6. _____ Cooking with oil can make you fat.

7. _____ The best pizza has just tomato sauce and lots of cheese.

8. _____ Foods like beans, rice, and potatoes should be eaten at every meal.

9. _____ Onions are good cooked and uncooked.

10. _____ I like a lot of salt in my food.

Part 4   Speaking

Talking About Recipes

1 **Discussing Recipes**

1. Work in groups of three. Each person chooses a different a recipe card (Recipe A, Recipe B, or Recipe C from pages 170–171). Do not look at the recipe cards of the other two people in your group.

2. First, ask and answer questions to get the missing ingredients.

3. Then, ask and answer questions to get the missing steps for making stuffed green peppers.

4. When you have all the steps, put them in the correct order.

   Example

   Student A: What ingredients do you have?

   Student B: I have 2 tablespoons chopped onion.

   Student C: I have 1 pound hamburger. What ingredients do you have?

Student A

Recipe for Stuffed Peppers

Ingredients
6 large green peppers
3/4 cup shredded cheese
_____   _____
_____   _____
_____   _____

Steps
• Stuff each pepper with hamburger mixture.
• Cook peppers in boiling water for 5 minutes.
• Sprinkle with shredded cheese.
_____
_____
_____
_____
_____

Student B

Recipe for Stuffed Peppers

Ingredients
2 tablespoons chopped onion
1 can tomato sauce
1 teaspoon salt
_____   _____
_____   _____
_____   _____

Steps
• Slice off top of each pepper.
• Cover and cook in oven at 450°F for 45 minutes.
• Cook and stir hamburger and onion until hamburger is
  light brown.
_____
_____
_____
_____
_____
_____

Student C

Recipe for Stuffed Peppers

Ingredients
1 pound hamburger
1/8 teaspoon garlic salt
1 cup cooked rice
_____
_____
_____

_____
_____
_____
_____
_____
_____

Steps
• Remove seeds from peppers.
• Stir in garlic, salt, rice, and one cup of the tomato sauce.
• Pour remaining tomato sauce over over peppers.
_____
_____
_____
_____
_____

2 Writing a Recipe Think about a dish that you can cook. Write some notes about how to cook it and list the ingredients. Then write the steps to prepare it.

Ingredients	Steps
_____	What do you do first? _____
_____	_____
_____	_____
_____	Next? _____
_____	_____
_____	_____
_____	Next? _____
_____	_____
_____	_____
_____	Next? _____
_____	_____
_____	_____

In groups of four, take turns presenting your dish. Tell the other students how to prepare it.

Talking About Nutrition

3 Discussing Contents of Food Talk in a group of four or five. Which of the following do you think about when you decide what to eat?

calories	cholesterol	protein	sugar
carbohydrates	fat	salt	vitamins

4 Comparing Food Labels Bring in a label from some food that you eat—a box, bag, or can. In groups, compare your labels. Which food has the most/least of the following ingredients? Complete the chart as you talk.

calories　　fat　　protein　　sodium　　sugar　　vitamins

Food	Has the Most . . .	Has the Least . . .
potato chips	sodium	vitamins

Self-Assessment Log

Check the words and expressions that you learned in this chapter.

Nouns
- ❑ an order of
- ❑ calories
- ❑ carrot
- ❑ charge
- ❑ cheese grater
- ❑ cucumber
- ❑ diet
- ❑ hot tea
- ❑ Italian dressing
- ❑ maître d'
- ❑ mushroom
- ❑ onion soup
- ❑ ounce
- ❑ picnic
- ❑ produce
- ❑ teaspoon
- ❑ vegetarian

Verbs
- ❑ beat
- ❑ brown
- ❑ chop
- ❑ decide
- ❑ grate
- ❑ order

Adjectives
- ❑ diet
- ❑ good/bad for you
- ❑ worried about

Adverb
- ❑ thoroughly

Expression
- ❑ You said it!

Check the things you did in this chapter. How well can you do each one?

	Very well	Fairly Well	Not very well
I can listen for the main ideas.	❑	❑	❑
I can listen for specific information.	❑	❑	❑
I can guess the meanings of words from context.	❑	❑	❑
I can identify stress and reductions.	❑	❑	❑
I can understand instructions and recipes.	❑	❑	❑
I can categorize vocabulary words.	❑	❑	❑
I can use my Internet search skills to find information about food.	❑	❑	❑
I can talk about recipes and nutrition.	❑	❑	❑
I can put steps of a recipe in order.	❑	❑	❑
I can order in a restaurant.	❑	❑	❑
I can talk about food and nutrition.	❑	❑	❑

Write about what you learned and what you did in this chapter.

In this chapter,

I learned _____

_____

I liked _____

_____

9

Great Destinations

❝ No man should travel until he has learned the language of the country he visits. ❞

—Ralph Waldo Emerson,
U.S. author, poet, and philosopher (1803–1882)

Connecting to the Topic

1 Who are these people? What are they doing?

2 What kinds of activities do you think they are doing on their trip?

3 Where have you traveled to? What kinds of activities have you done in your travels?

Part 1

Conversation: Arriving in
San Francisco

Before You Listen

 1 Prelistening Questions Look at the photos and answer the questions
with a classmate.

▲ Photo 1

▲ Photo 2

1. Look at Photo 1. What city is this? How do you know?

2. Look at Photo 2. What city is this? What do you know about this city? Where is
this city? How's the weather there? What is it like in the winter? What is it like
in the summer? What are some things you can see and do there?

3. Do you like to visit big cities? Why or why not?

4. What interesting places in your country have you visited or do you know about?

5. What place around the world would you most like to visit? Why?

6. Do you prefer to fly, drive, or take the train when you travel? Why?

 2 Vocabulary Preview It is spring break. Dan, Beth, and Ali are driving to San
Francisco. They are just now arriving in the city. Listen to these words and expressions
from their conversation. Check (✓) the ones that you know.

Nouns	Verbs	Adjective
❑ criminal	❑ change (a tire)	❑ triangular
❑ flat tire	❑ explore	**Expression**
❑ landmark	❑ pull over	❑ can't wait
❑ prison		
❑ skyline		
❑ spare tire		
❑ tower		

3 **Guessing the Meanings of New Words from Context** Guess the meanings of the underlined words. Write your guesses on the lines. Check your answers with a dictionary or with your teacher.

1. New York's <u>skyline</u> is world famous. You can see many tall buildings and the Statue of Liberty.

My guess: _____

2. A car has five tires: one on each wheel and one called a <u>spare tire</u>.

My guess: _____

3. My car has a <u>flat tire</u>. I think there's a hole in it.

My guess: _____

4. I'm going to <u>pull over</u> to the side of the road and stop the car.

My guess: _____

5. I had to <u>change</u> the flat tire. Now I need to buy a new tire to replace the spare tire.

My guess: _____

6. The pyramids in Egypt have <u>triangular</u> sides.

My guess: _____

7. Bonnie and Clyde were famous American <u>criminals</u> who lived in the 1920s. They robbed a lot of banks and killed several people.

My guess: _____

8. After the man robbed a bank, he was put in <u>prison</u> for six years.

My guess: _____

9. My family and I are going to Disneyland next month. My kids <u>can't wait</u> to meet Mickey Mouse!

My guess: _____

10. London's Big Ben and the Eiffel Tower in Paris are famous <u>landmarks</u>.

My guess: _____

11. Ali: What's that tall building over there?

Beth: It's not a building. It's a water <u>tower</u>. It holds fresh water.

My guess: _____

12. I love to <u>explore</u> interesting cities for the first time. I look for good restaurants, new stores for shopping, and places with good nightlife.

My guess: _____

4 **Listening for Main Ideas (Part 1)** Listen to the first part of the conversation. Choose the best answer to each question.

1. What are Dan, Beth, and Ali enjoying?
- (A) visiting San Francisco
- (B) looking at the San Francisco skyline
- (C) the tour of Alcatraz

2. What is the Transamerica Building?
- (A) a San Francisco landmark and part of the San Francisco skyline
- (B) a triangular tower
- (C) both a and b

3. What is Alcatraz?
- (A) a prison where dangerous criminals are put
- (B) a former prison and an interesting place to tour
- (C) a famous bridge

5 **Listening for Main Ideas (Part 2)** Now listen to the whole conversation. Choose the best answer to each question.

1. What does Dan say he wants to do tomorrow?
- (A) visit Alcatraz
- (B) see all of San Francisco's famous landmarks
- (C) change the flat tire

2. Why does Dan pull the car over?
- (A) because the car has a flat tire
- (B) because they (Dan, Beth, and Ali) need to get to San Francisco
- (C) because they want to visit Alcatraz

3. What does Ali say about the flat tire?
- (A) It will take a long time to change it.
- (B) It will take a short time to change it.
- (C) Dan and Beth can change it.

▲ Beth

▲ Ali

▲ Dan

6 **Listening for Specific Information** Listen again. Choose best answer to each question.

1. Ali says, "I can't wait to go to all those places". What does he mean?
   - (A) He's excited about visiting San Francisco's famous landmarks.
   - (B) He's going to visit San Francisco's famous landmarks today.
   - (C) He wants to visit just Alcatraz.

2. What does Dan want to do tomorrow?
   - (A) visit Alcatraz all day
   - (B) visit Alcatraz, perhaps in the morning or the afternoon
   - (C) visit all of San Francisco's landmarks

3. How long will it take to change the flat tire?
   - (A) A few minutes
   - (B) All afternoon
   - (C) A day

After You Listen

Strategy

Using a Graphic Organizer: T-charts

To compare two things, you can make a graphic organizer called a T-chart. For example, you can compare two places by using a T-chart. Label one column with one place and the other column with the other place. Write words describing each place below the labels. Group the negative words and the positive words. A T-chart can help you choose which place is better. The T-chart below compares two places: the beach and the mountains. You will practice making a T-chart to compare two places in Activity 7.

The Beach	The Mountains
warm	cold
sand	snow
water	ice
vacation place	vacation place
swimming	skiing
bathing suit	coat

7 **Using a T-chart to Compare Two Places** Work with a partner. Decide which of the words in the box below describe San Francisco, California. Decide which of the words in the box describe the Grand Canyon. Some words may describe both places. Write the words in the appropriate column on the T-chart. Add a few words of your own.

▲ San Francisco

▲ Grand Canyon

beautiful	dry	lively	peaceful	uncrowded
calm	exciting	modern	rugged	wild
colorful	famous	natural		

San Francisco	Grand Canyon

Now look at the T-chart and compare San Francisco to the Grand Canyon. Answer this question with your partner.

Which place would you like to visit? Why?

With your partner, think of two places you would like to visit. Make a T-chart like the one above comparing your two places.

Stress

8 Listening for Stressed Words Listen to the first part of the conversation again. Some of the stressed words are missing. Fill in the blanks with words from the box. Some words may be used more than once.

ahead	Francisco's	skyline	triangular
almost	landmarks	tall	wait
Bridge	Look	That's	
famous	looks	There's	
Francisco	places	tower	

Beth: _____, guys, up ahead! _____ San
_____1_____ _____2_____

_____! We're almost there!
_____3_____

Ali: _____ at that _____! What's that _____,
_____4_____ _____5_____ _____6_____

_____ building? It _____ like a _____.
_____7_____ _____8_____ _____9_____

Dan: _____ the Transamerica Building. It's one of San
_____10_____

_____ _____. It's _____ as
_____11_____ _____12_____ _____13_____

_____ now as the Golden Gate _____, the cable cars,
_____14_____ _____15_____

Chinatown . . .

Ali: Well, I can't _____ to go to all those _____ . . . and
_____16_____ _____17_____

Alcatraz, too.

Now read the conversation in a group of three. Practice stressing words.

WORD FAMILIES AND STRESS

A word family is a group of related nouns, verbs, adjectives, or adverbs. For example, *photograph, photography, photographic.* The different words in a word family have different stress.

Examples

photógraphy (n)	phótograph (n and v)	photográphic (adj)
educátion (n)	éducate (v)	educátional (adj)
examinátion (n)	exámine (v)	
récord (n)	recórd (v)	
biógraphy (n)		biográphical (adj)

9 **Stress and Word Families** Listen to the word families below, Repeat each word after the speaker.

1. photógraphy (n)   phótograph (n and v)   photográphic (adj)

2. récord (n)   recórd (v)

3. désert (n)   desért (v)   desérted (adj)

4. bénefit (n)   bénefit (v)   benefícial (adj)

5. biógraphy (n)   biográphical (adj)

6. análysis (n)   ánalyze (v)   analýtical (adj)

7. examinátion (n)   exámine (v)

8. educátion (n)   éducate (v)   educátional (adj)

10 **Listening for Stress** Listen to the sentences. Mark the stress of the underlined word.

1. Photography is a popular hobby.

2. The desert is a bad place to have a flat tire.

3. I keep good records of my income and expenses.

4. The medicine had a beneficial effect on the patient.

5. I have class tonight, so please record my favorite TV program for me.

6. You must pass the examination to pass the course.

7. Schools try to educate every student equally.

8. I need to analyze the results of my research.

9. I read Ulysses Grant's biography for my history course.

10. Please take a photograph of us in front of the monument.

Using the Internet

Finding Photos on the Internet

Photographs can give you a great deal of information. They can help you understand new ideas. Photos are also useful for learning about new places and for planning travel.

Here's one way to find photos on the Internet: Go to a search engine. Click on "Images." Into the text box, type keywords that describe the pictures you want.

Example

| Grand Canyon | Submit |

Use the keyword and search skills that you learned in this book.

11 **Practicing Your Search Skills** Practice looking for photos on the Internet. Look for photos of places. Try to find photos of the following. If possible, print your photos and bring them to class.

- San Francisco
- the Grand Canyon
- a famous landmark
- your favorite place to visit
- a place you would like to visit

Discuss your results with the class.

1. What keyword combinations did you use?

2. Did you check the URLs before you went to the site?

3. Who found the best photos?

Talk It Over

12 **Describing Photos** Look at the photos below. Describe one of the photos to your group. Don't tell them which photo you are describing. Your group will guess which photo you are describing.

Example Many people visit this place every year to ski.

▲ Photo 1

▲ Photo 2

▲ Photo 3

▲ Photo 4

Persuading Others

EXPRESSIONS FOR PERSUADING OTHERS

When you talk to people at work, at school, and in other places, you often want to convince them to do something. This is called *persuasion*. The vocabulary list in Activity 1 shows some expressions you can use to persuade other people.

Before You Listen

1 Vocabulary Preview You are going to hear a conversation consisting of suggestions and persuasion. Listen to these words and expressions from the conversation. Check (✓) the ones that you know.

Noun	Verb	Expressions	
❏ the way back	❏ should	❏ Couldn't we . . .	❏ Sounds good/OK
		❏ I'd rather . . .	❏ Wouldn't you
		❏ Let's	rather . . .

Listen

2 Listening for Main Ideas
Listen to the conversations. Number the photos to match Conversation 1, Conversation 2, or Conversation 3.

3 Listening for Specific Information Listen to the conversations again and fill in the chart below. Where do Ali, Beth, and Ming want to go? What reasons do they give?

Person	Place They Want to Go	Reasons They Give
Ali		
Beth		
Ming		

After You Listen

WAYS MEN AND WOMEN PERSUADE OTHERS

Some experts say that in the United States, men usually use statements to make suggestions or to persuade. For example, in the conversations in Activity 2, Lee, Ali, and Dan made these statements:

Lee: Ali, it's a perfect day to go to the beach. **Let's go!**

Ali: I'd rather go on a bike ride. **Come and ride up** to the Prospect Park Lake with me.

Dan: There's a new Mexican restaurant on Poplar. **Let's go** there.

On the other hand, women often ask questions or use words such as *could* and *would*. For example, in the conversations in Activity 2, Alicia, Beth, and Ming say:

Alicia: Hey, Beth. **Do you want to go** shopping at the mall today?

Beth: I think I've been spending too much money lately. **Wouldn't you rather go** for a nice walk in the mountains?

Ming: Oh, I ate there last night. It was a little too spicy for me. **Couldn't we go** to Wang's instead?

4 How Do You Persuade Others? In small groups, discuss the following questions. Report your discussion to the class.

1. In your native language, do you think that men and women use different ways to persuade others?

2. If you are a woman, do you usually make statements or ask questions to persuade someone? If you are a man, do you usually make statements or ask questions to persuade someone? Discuss with your group.

EXPRESSIONS FOR MAKING SUGGESTIONS AND EXPRESSING OPINIONS

The following expressions will help you make suggestions and give your opinion.

Making Suggestions

Let's go	(to the beach.)
We could go	(swimming.)
Would you like to go	(to a lake?)
Wouldn't you like to go	(camping?)
Would you rather go	(to a big city?)
Wouldn't you rather go	(sightseeing?)

Expressing Opinions

I'd like to go	(to the mountains.)
I don't like to go	(fishing.)
I'd rather go	(waterskiing.)

5 Persuading Others

1. In a small group, plan a trip you want to take together. Choose a place from the photos below or choose your own idea. Persuade the people in your group to go there. Use the expressions in the box above and the words in the boxes below.

2. As a group, choose the most exciting trip.

3. When you finish, tell the class where your group is going and why.

Trip #1: To the beach
Activities:
Swimming
Sunbathing
Walking in the sand

Trip #2: To a lake in the mountains
Activities:
Fishing
Boating and waterskiing
Hiking

Trip #3: To a big city
Activities:
Sightseeing
Shopping
Dining out
Going to the museums

Trip #4: To an amusement park
Activities:
Riding the roller coaster
Playing games for prizes
Seeing shows

Trip #5: To the countryside
Activities:
Driving
Eating
Exploring
Walking

Trip #6: [Your idea]
Activities:

▲ Draw a picture here.

Getting Meaning from Context

 1 Vocabulary Preview Dan, Beth, and Ali are on another trip. This time they are in the southwestern United States. Listen to these words and expressions from their conversation. Check (✓) the ones that you know.

Nouns
- ❑ advisory
- ❑ fishing equipment
- ❑ flash flood
- ❑ luggage

- ❑ sleeping bag
- ❑ tent
- ❑ trunk

Verb
- ❑ take up space

Adjective
- ❑ freezing

▲ Driving through New Mexico in the southwestern United States.

▲ Beth

▲ Ali

▲ Dan

2 **Using Context Clues** You will hear five conversations. Listen to each conversation and choose the best answer. Continue to listen to check each answer.

1. What did Beth, Dan, and Ali finish doing?
   - (A) changing a flat tire
   - (B) putting everything in the car
   - (C) taking everything out of the car

2. What are Beth, Dan, and Ali going to do?
   - (A) eat a picnic lunch in the desert
   - (B) look at a map
   - (C) find a restaurant

3. Why is Dan going to turn on the radio?
   - (A) to listen to some music
   - (B) to hear a weather report
   - (C) to find something to listen to

4. What's the weather probably going to be like tonight?
   - (A) rainy and hot
   - (B) cloudy and cool
   - (C) rainy and cold

5. Why is Dan sorry?
   - (A) He didn't listen to the weather report.
   - (B) He didn't want to go camping in the rain.
   - (C) He didn't see a stop sign.

Listening to a Tour Guide

Before You Listen

3 **Preparing to Listen** Before you listen, talk about sightseeing with a partner.

1. Do you like to go sightseeing?

2. What kinds of places do you like to visit?

3. What city in the world do you think is good for sightseeing?

4. What is your favorite sight to see in your hometown or your city?

5. What are some other sights in your hometown or your city?

4 Vocabulary Preview Match the words and expressions with the photos below. Look at the example.

1. __b__ interstate highway
2. _____ capitol building
3. _____ Civil War general

4. _____ amusement park
5. _____ fountain
6. _____ graves

a.

b.

c.

d.

e.

f.

Listen

5 Listening for Main Ideas You are going to go on a sightseeing tour of a major U.S. city. The tour guide is going to describe some interesting sights in the city. As you listen, answer these questions.

1. What state are you in? _____

2. What city are you touring? _____

6 Listening for Places on a Map Listen again. This time, look at the map of Atlanta as you listen. As you hear the description of each place, write the number of the place in the correct blank on the map.

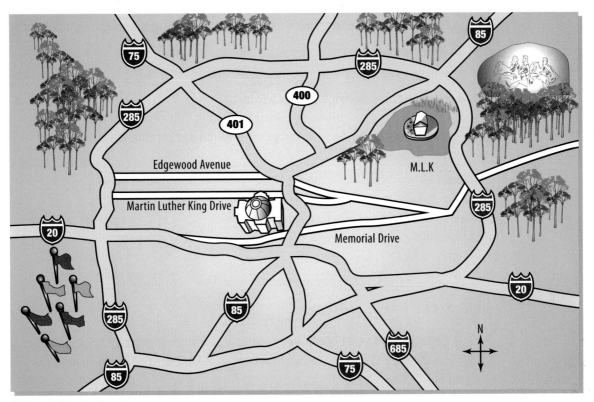

▲ Map of Atlanta, Georgia

 7 Listening for Details Listen again. Write a few notes next to each location describing the location.

The Capitol Building _____

_____

Martin Luther King, Jr. National Historic Site _____

_____

Stone Mountain _____

_____

Amusement Park _____

_____

Before You Listen

8 Preparing to Listen Before you listen, discuss these questions in small groups.

1. When did you last (most recently) take a plane trip?

2. Where did you go?

3. Did you enjoy the trip? Why or why not?

9 Vocabulary Preview Listen to these words and phrases. Check (✓) the ones that you know.

Nouns	Verbs	Adjectives
❑ business class	❑ arrive	❑ direct
❑ economy class	❑ change planes	❑ nonrefundable
❑ first class	❑ depart	❑ nonstop
❑ one way		❑ one way (ticket)
❑ round trip		❑ round trip (ticket)

Listen

10 Listening for the Main Idea Alicia is planning a trip to Walt Disney World in Florida. She goes to a travel agency to get some information. Listen and answer this question.

How will Alicia travel? Circle the number of the correct photo.

▲ Photo 1

▲ Photo 2

11 Listening for Specific Information Listen again and choose the best answer to each question.

1. What kind of ticket does Alicia want to buy?
   - (A) first class
   - (B) economy class
   - (C) business class

2. When does Alicia's flight leave?
   - (A) on Saturday afternoon
   - (B) on Sunday evening
   - (C) on Sunday morning

3. Why doesn't Alicia want the nonstop, direct flight?
   - (A) She wants to visit Atlanta.
   - (B) It's much more expensive.
   - (C) It takes longer.

4. Why is Alicia's ticket nonrefundable?
   - (A) It's a special low fare.
   - (B) It's nonstop.
   - (C) She's going economy.

After You Listen

 12 Discussing Flight Information Discuss the following questions in small groups.

1. Have you ever used a travel agent to plan a trip?

2. Which of the following would you rather do? Why?
   a. pay more for a nonstop flight (or express train) to arrive sooner
   b. pay more for a nonstop flight (or express train) so you don't have to change planes (or trains)
   c. save money by taking a longer flight (or trip) and changing planes (or trains)

3. How long in advance do you usually plan a trip?

▲ Passenger in an airplane

Planning a Trip

ASKING ABOUT FLIGHTS

Here are questions and expressions that will help you ask about flights.

Helpful Questions

How much is the fare from Atlanta to . . . ?

Does it make any stops?

What is the departure (arrival) time?

How many days before the flight do I buy the advance-purchase tickets?

Helpful Expressions

The fare is . . .

It makes . . . stop(s).

The departure (arrival) time is . . .

There are . . . days advance purchase.

 1 **Asking About Flights** Work in small groups. Practice saying the questions and expressions in the box above. Help each other with pronunciation.

 2 **Reading Flight Information**

1. Work with a partner. Student A looks at Chart A on this page.

2. Student B looks at Chart B on page 195.

3. Ask and answer questions you practiced in Activity 1.

4. Fill in the information on your charts.

5. Check your answers with your partner's chart.

Chart A					
From Atlanta to:					
City	**Fare**	**Stops**	**Departure Time**	**Arrival Time**	**Advance Purchase**
Chicago				12:47 P.M.	21 days
New York	$182	0	9:05 A.M.		21 days
Los Angeles	$349			1:21 P.M.	
San Francisco			9:00 A.M.		
Miami	$128	0		11:48 A.M.	
London		2	10:30 A.M.		21 days
Paris	$778			7:05 A.M.	
Tokyo			9:30 A.M.		
Vancouver		1			3 days

Chart B					
From Atlanta to:					
City	Fare	Stops	Departure Time	Arrival Time	Advance Purchase
Chicago	*$118*	*0*	*9:45 A.M.*		
New York				*11:12 A.M.*	
Los Angeles		*1*	*9:00 A.M.*		*3 days*
San Francisco	*$349*	*1*		*1:27 P.M.*	*3 days*
Miami			*9:55 A.M.*		*21 days*
London	*$738*			*6:35 P.M.*	
Paris		*0*	*1:30 P.M.*		*7 days*
Tokyo	*$1,340*	*0*		*3:25 P.M.*	*7 days*
Vancouver	*$385*		*4:32 P.M.*	*9:09 P.M.*	

3 **Getting Trip Information** Go to a travel agency. Get information on a trip you would like to take. Report to the class on the airfare and the times of the flights.

Discussing Travel

4 **Describing Trip Destinations** Work in small groups. Think of five interesting places to see in your area. Prepare a short description of each place. Tell your descriptions to the class, but don't give the names of the places. Can the class guess the places you are describing?

5 **Talking About Travel** Travel is very popular, and people like to talk about it. Pick one trip you took and tell the class something about it. Plan your talk by making notes in the chart on page 196.

Questions	Notes
What is the name of the place you went?	
Who did you go with?	
When did you go? How long did you stay?	
What did you visit?	
What special activities did you do?	
What foods did you eat?	
What was the best part of the trip?	

6 **Reading About Travel in the Newspaper** Find a story about travel in an English language newspaper. Read the story. Write three new words from the story on the lines below. Tell the class the three new words you learned.

_____

_____

_____

Self-Assessment Log

Check the words and expressions that you learned in this chapter.

Nouns

- ❏ advisory
- ❏ business class
- ❏ coach class
- ❏ criminal
- ❏ first class
- ❏ fishing equipment
- ❏ flash flood
- ❏ flat tire
- ❏ landmark
- ❏ luggage
- ❏ one way
- ❏ prison
- ❏ round trip
- ❏ skyline
- ❏ sleeping bag

- ❏ spare tire
- ❏ tent
- ❏ the way back
- ❏ tower
- ❏ trunk

Verbs

- ❏ arrive
- ❏ change (a tire)
- ❏ change planes
- ❏ depart
- ❏ explore
- ❏ pull over
- ❏ should
- ❏ take up space

Adjectives

- ❏ direct
- ❏ freezing
- ❏ nonrefundable
- ❏ nonstop
- ❏ one way (ticket)
- ❏ round trip (ticket)
- ❏ triangular

Idioms and Expressions

- ❏ can't wait
- ❏ Couldn't we. . .
- ❏ I'd rather. . .
- ❏ Let's
- ❏ Sounds good/OK
- ❏ Wouldn't you rather. . .

Check the things you did in this chapter. How well can you do each one?

	Very well	Fairly well	Not very well
I can listen for the main ideas.	❏	❏	❏
I can listen for specific information.	❏	❏	❏
I can guess the meanings of words from context.	❏	❏	❏
I can listen for and understand stress and reductions.	❏	❏	❏
I can use a T-chart to compare two places.	❏	❏	❏
I can understand flight information.	❏	❏	❏
I can understand a tour guide.	❏	❏	❏
I can use my Internet search skills to find photos.	❏	❏	❏
I can persuade others.	❏	❏	❏
I can ask for travel information.	❏	❏	❏
I can talk about travel.	❏	❏	❏

Write about what you learned and what you did in this chapter.

In this chapter,

I learned _____

_____

I liked _____

_____

Our Planet

In This Chapter

Using Language: Expressing Opinions
Listening: Listening to Persuasive Messages
Speaking: Talking About Endangered Species

❝ Earth provides enough to satisfy every man's need but not every man's greed. ❞

—Mahatma Gandhi
Indian spiritual and political leader (1869–1948)

Connecting to the Topic

1. Describe what Alicia and Lee are doing.

2. What is Earth Day?

3. What are some environmental problems in the world?

Before You Listen

1 **Prelistening Questions** Look at the following sunray graphic organizer. Discuss the questions below with a classmate. Then, write on the T-chart below some of the causes of the problems and some of the solutions.

▲ Water pollution

▲ Car pollution

▲ Air pollution

1. What planet is in the center of the graphic organizer above?

2. What are some of the problems shown on the graphic organizer above?

3. What are the causes (reasons) for these problems? Fill in the "causes" column of the T-chart below with your group.

4. What do you think people need to do to solve (answer) these problems? Fill in the "Solutions" column of the T-chart below.

Causes of Pollution	Solutions
Cars	Use fewer cars/more bicycles

2 Vocabulary Preview Lee is visiting Alicia in her dorm (dormitory) room. Listen to these words and expressions from their conversation. Check (✓) the ones that you know.

Nouns
❑ campus
❑ environment
❑ exhibit
❑ pollution
❑ student union

Verbs
❑ give a speech
❑ plant
❑ pollute
❑ support

Expression
❑ a lot going on

3 Guessing the Meaning of Words Guess the meanings of the underlined words. Write your guesses on the lines. Check your answers with a dictionary or your teacher.

1. Today the air in many cities is very dirty. Cars and factories cause this air <u>pollution</u>.

   My guess: _____

2. We live on the earth. It is our natural <u>environment</u>.

   My guess: _____

3. I'm going to <u>give a speech</u> to the class. I'm going to talk about the planet and pollution in front of the class.

   My guess: _____

4. People don't want cars and factories to <u>pollute</u> the air. We need clean, not dirty, air.

   My guess: _____

5. The Faber College <u>campus</u> is small but very nice: it has lots of outdoor places where students can study or just relax.

   My guess: _____

6. Art museums have <u>exhibits</u> of paintings or other art that people can look at.

   My guess: _____

7. Many colleges and universities have a <u>student union</u> where students can meet, get something to eat, shop, or just spend their free time.

   My guess: _____

8. I want the water and air to be clean, so I <u>support</u> Earth Day.

   My guess: _____

9. My mother's hobby is gardening: she loves to <u>plant</u> flowers and take care of them.

   My guess: _____

10. There's always a <u>lot going on</u> in a big city like London: shows, concerts, nightlife, exhibits, and other events.

    My guess: _____

4 **Listening for Main Ideas** Listen to the first part of the conversation. Choose the best answer to each question.

1. What is Alicia doing?

(A) She's studying about Earth Day.

(B) She's making a sign for Earth Day.

(C) She's thinking about pollution.

2. On Earth Day, what do people think about?

(A) the first Earth Day in 1970

(B) problems with the environment

(C) clean air and water

3. When is Earth Day?

(A) in 1970

(B) the last Monday in April

(C) April 22nd

5 **Listening for Specific Information (Part 1)** Now listen to the whole conversation. Choose the best answer to each question.

1. What do people talk and learn about on Earth Day?

(A) Washington, D.C.

(B) the Earth and the environment

(C) riding their bicycles

2. When did Earth Day start?

(A) last year

(B) last April 22nd

(C) more than 30 years ago

3. What kinds of things do people think about on Earth Day?

(A) air and pollution

(B) clean energy

(C) both a and b

4. What are Alicia and Lee going to do on Earth Day?

(A) give a speech and carry signs

(B) go to Washington, D.C.

(C) plant some trees

▲ "I'm making a sign for Earth Day."

6 Listening for Specific Information (Part 2) Listen again. Choose the best answer to each question.

1. What Earth Day activity happened one year?
   - (A) One thousand people came to Washington, D.C. to support pollution.
   - (B) People in 150 towns in Italy didn't use their cars.
   - (C) Students at Faber College planted trees around the student union.

2. What's going on at Faber College next Monday?
   - (A) There will be exhibits at the student union.
   - (B) Alicia will give a speech about pollution.
   - (C) both a and b

3. What does Lee say he wants to do on Earth Day?
   - (A) give a speech
   - (B) carry a sign
   - (C) plant trees

After You Listen

7 Vocabulary Review Complete the sentences below. Use words from the list.

be going on	exhibit	pollution	support
campus	give a speech	student union	to plant
environment	pollute		

1. Cars are one of the biggest causes of air _____.

2. After class, Beth and Ali are going to have some coffee at the

   _____.

3. I want to tell people about Earth Day, but I'm afraid to

   _____ in public.

4. Some factories _____ the air more than others.

5. Alicia and Lee _____ Earth Day because they want clean air and water.

6. What laws do we need to protect the _____ from air and water pollution?

7. The _____ at Faber College is small but very nice. It has a lot of grass and trees.

8. Many people are going _____ trees on Earth Day.

9. What will _____ in your country on Earth Day?

10. There's a special _____ about Earth day at the local art museum.

Stress

8 Listening for Stressed Words Listen to the first part of the conversation again. Some of the words in the box below are stressed. Fill in the blanks with the words from the box. Some words will be used more than once.

April	fine	Monday	sign
busy	going	people	that
doing	Hi	pollution	think
Earth Day	in	problems	year
environment	is	Really	

Alicia: Come _____!
                      1

Lee: _____, Alicia. How's it _____?
                      2   3

Alicia: _____, Lee. I'm _____ . . . but _____.
                      4   5   6

Lee: What are you _____?
                                        7

Alicia: I'm making a _____ for _____.
                                    8   9

Lee: *Earth* Day? What's _____?
                                              10

Alicia: On Earth Day, people _____ about _____.
                                                        11   12

and other _____ with the _____.
                            13   14

Lee: _____! When is _____?
                      15   16

Alicia: Next _____.
                              17

Lee: . . . and is it every _____?
                                              18

Alicia: Yes, it _____. The first Earth Day was in 1970, and it now
                              19

happens every _____, on _____ 22nd.
                                  20   21

On _____ day, _____ talk and learn
              22   23

about _____ with the _____.
                    24   25

Now read the conversation with a partner. Practice stressing words.

Emphasis

EMPHASIS AND MEANING

The same sentence can have different meanings if different words are emphasized or stressed. For example, listen to the following conversations.

Conversation 1

Alicia: At the student union, there will be exhibits on pollution. Students will also plant some trees around the college campus.

Lee: So what are *you* going to do on Earth Day?

Alicia: I'm going to give a speech.

Lee is asking about *Alicia's* plans compared to what other people do on Earth Day.

Conversation 2

Alicia: I usually visit my family on special days like Thanksgiving and New Year's.

Lee: So what are you going to do on *Earth Day*?

Alicia: I'm going to give a speech at the student union.

Lee is asking about Alicia's plans for *Earth Day* compared to other special days.

Conversation 3

Alicia: I think about pollution on Earth Day, and I worry about the environment.

Lee: So what are you planning to *do* on Earth Day?

Alicia: I'm going to give a speech and carry a sign.

Lee is asking about Alicia's *actions* compared to her thoughts.

9 Listening for Emphasis Listen to sentences in the following conversations. Circle the letter of the sentence that you hear.

1. a. What do *you* think about pollution?
   b. What do you think about *pollution*?

2. a. Do you think *air pollution* is the biggest problem?
   b. Do you think air pollution is the *biggest* problem?

3. a. Will you ride your *bicycle* to school on Earth Day?
   b. Will you ride your bicycle to *school* on Earth Day?

4. a. How *many* trees will you plant on campus?
   b. How many trees will you plant on *campus*?

5. a. *Which* park are you going to clean up?
   b. Which park are *you* going to clean up?

Using the Internet

Finding News

The Internet is one of the best ways to get current news. Websites such as Yahoo and Google have news. Newspapers and TV networks also have websites with the latest news.

To get news on the Internet, go to a site such as www.google.com and click on the News section. Then type a topic into the text box.

Example

| Air pollution | Submit |

10 **Practicing Your Search Skills** Look for the latest news on one of the following topics. Use the keyword and search skills that you learned in this book. Print your news stories. If possible, find pictures on your topic and bring them to class.

- Earth Day
- air or water pollution
- ways to help save the environment
- environmental organizations in your community
- celebrities (actors, musicians, etc.) who are involved in saving the environment
- your idea

Discuss your results with the class.

1. What keyword combinations did you use?

2. Did you check the URLs before you went to the site?

3. Who found the most interesting and recent stories?

Talk It Over

11 **Understanding Emphasis in Questions** Work with a partner. Look at the following conversations. Decide how Alicia would respond. Pay attention to the emphasis in Lee's questions. What information does he want? The teacher may ask you to perform your conversations for the class.

Alicia: Some people think air pollution is a big problem, but others think progress is more important.

Lee: Well, what do *you* think about pollution?

Alicia: _____

_____

Alicia: Air pollution and water pollution are two serious environmental problems.

Lee: Do you think *air pollution* is the biggest problem?

Alicia: _____

_____

Alicia: One of the things I do on Earth Day is to stop driving my car.

Lee: Will you ride your *bicycle* to school on Earth Day?

Alicia: _____

_____

Alicia: We're going to plant trees all over town on Earth Day. We have 500 trees to plant.

Lee: How many trees will you plant on *campus*?

Alicia: _____

_____

Alicia: Students from the college are going to clean up Audubon Park, Haley Park, Finley Park, and Tom Lee Park.

Lee: Which park are *you* going to clean up?

Alicia: _____

_____

Part 2 Using Language

Expressing Opinions

AGREEING AND DISAGREEING

People often have different opinions or ideas on a topic. You can have interesting conversations with people who don't agree with you. But if you give your opinion in the wrong way, people might think you are being rude. Here are some expressions to use when you agree or disagree in a conversation. Repeat them after your teacher.

To Agree	To Disagree
That's a good point.	You have a point, but . . .
I agree with you.	I'm afraid I don't agree with you on that.
You're right.	That may be true, but I think . . .
I feel the same way.	In my opinion, . . .
Of course, . . .	I understand your point of view, but . . .

1 Listening for Main Ideas Amy and Nabil are having a discussion. As you listen, answer these questions.

1. What are they talking about?

2. Do they have the same opinion, or do they disagree?

▲ Cars are one of the causes of air pollution.

 2 Listening for Opinions Listen again. This time, pay attention to the expressions of disagreement. Circle the words you hear.

Amy: Air pollution is so bad in this city! I think the local government should stop people from driving cars on certain days.

Nabil: You (have a point / had a point). Air pollution *is* a problem, but not letting people drive on certain days is a bad idea. People need their cars to get to work, and trucks need to deliver goods to stores.

Amy: I'm afraid I (agree / don't agree) with you there. Saving the environment is (so / too) important. People are so used to driving that they don't think of other ways to do things. If we stopped people from driving on certain days, maybe we could think of new ways to get around.

Nabil: I understand (you / your point of view), but I still think it wouldn't be possible to stop people from driving.

1. As a class, choose a topic from the chart below and divide into two teams. Your teacher will help you decide which side of the topic your team will debate.

2. Line up chairs in two facing rows as in the picture.

SIDE A 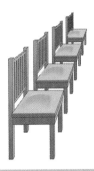  **SIDE B**

3. First a student on one side states an opinion for his or her team.

4. Then a student on the other side states an opinion. Use the expressions of agreement and disagreement. Continue until each student has had a turn.

5. Your teacher will give a point to each student who uses one of the expressions. The team with the most points at the end wins.

Topics	
Side A	**Side B**
1. The government should *not* permit people to drive cars in cities.	The government *should* permit people to drive cars in cities.
2. The government should permit parents to have *more than one* child.	The government should permit parents to have *only one* child.
3. Students should *only* study in school; they *shouldn't* play sports.	Students *need* sports in school; they *should do more than* only study.
4. People *should* be able to smoke in public places such as restaurants.	People *should not* be able to smoke in public places such as restaurants.

▲ Students should not play sports in school. They should only study.

▲ Students need sports. They should play sports in school.

Part 3 | Listening

Getting Meaning from Context

1 Using Context Clues You will hear five speakers. Listen to each speaker. Write the number of the speaker next to the best answer below. Continue to listen to check each answer.

_____ air pollution   _____ overcrowding (too many people)

_____ crime   _____ the environment

_____ water pollution

Listening to Persuasive Messages

Before You Listen

2 Preparing to Listen Before you listen, discuss these questions in a small group.

1. What do people do in their everyday lives to contribute to pollution and other environmental problems?

2. Do you personally do anything to help the environment?

3 Vocabulary Preview Listen to these words and phrases. Check (✓) the ones that you know.

Nouns
- ❏ carbon dioxide
- ❏ endangered species
- ❏ faucet
- ❏ recyclables
- ❏ shuttle bus
- ❏ topsoil
- ❏ toxic chemicals

Verb
- ❏ recycle

Adjectives
- ❏ mature
- ❏ slaughtered
- ❏ veggie (vegetable or vegetarian)

Listen

4 Listening for the Main Idea (Part 1) Listen to the following messages. As you listen, answer this question.

Where might you hear these messages?

5 Listening for Main Ideas (Part 2) Listen again. This time, write the number of the message next to the main idea of the message.

a. _____ Save water.

b. _____ Don't eat meat.

c. _____ Don't drive your car.

d. _____ Recycle—don't throw things away.

e. _____ Eat food without chemicals.

6 Listening for Details Listen again. This time, match each of the main messages with the details about how you can help or hurt the environment. There may be more than one detail for each main message.

Main Message

1. Save water
2. Don't eat meat.
3. Don't drive your car.
4. Recycle, don't throw things away.
5. Eat food without chemicals.

Details

a. Raising cattle for meat uses a lot of water, topsoil, and other resources.

b. It's better to recycle your trash than to throw it away.

c. Cars pollute the air.

d. Animals raised for meat contain toxic chemicals.

e. Trees produce oxygen to replace polluted air.

f. Raising cattle for meat adds carbon dioxide to the air.

g. Turn the water off while you brush your teeth.

h. Burgers made from vegetables are better for the environment than burgers made from meat.

i. Chemicals used to kill bugs on vegetables can cause cancer.

j. Cars cause noise pollution on city streets.

After You Listen

7 **Discussing Main Ideas** Answer these questions in small groups.

1. Do you agree with any of the main messages from the announcements at the Earth Fair? Which ones?

2. If you disagree with any of the main messages, tell your group why you disagree.

3. Do the members of your group do anything to help the environment? On the chart, list what actions you do in each of the following areas.

Goals	Actions Your Group Takes
1. Reduce air pollution from cars	
2. Save water	
3. Recycle glass, paper, cans, etc.	
4. Reduce use of toxic chemicals	
5. Other environmental issues	

Talking About Endangered Species

1 **Reading About Endangered Species** Read the passage below.

The Endangered Species List

Since the year 1600, more than 100 different kinds of animals have become extinct. That is, those animals don't exist anymore. We will never see another of those animals alive. Many more types of animals will disappear if they are not saved. These animals are called "endangered species."

Endangered species are protected from hunting and other threats. Sometimes, animals are taken off the endangered species list because they have become more numerous. The American grizzly bear is one example of success.

▲ An American grizzly bear

2 **Locating Endangered Species on a Map**

1. Work with a partner. Decide which one of you is Student A and which is Student B.

2. Student A should look at Map A on page 214. Student B should look at Map B on page 215.

3. Each map indicates a different endangered species. Ask your partner questions so you can fill in the missing information on your map. When you are finished, check your maps.

Example

Student A (looking at Map A): What animal is endangered in North America?

Student B (looking at Map B): The American alligator.

Map A

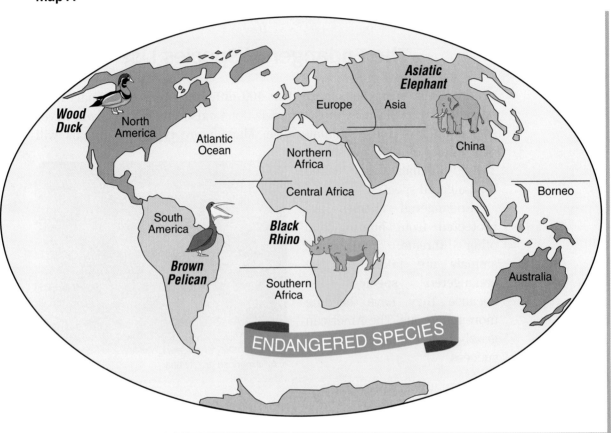

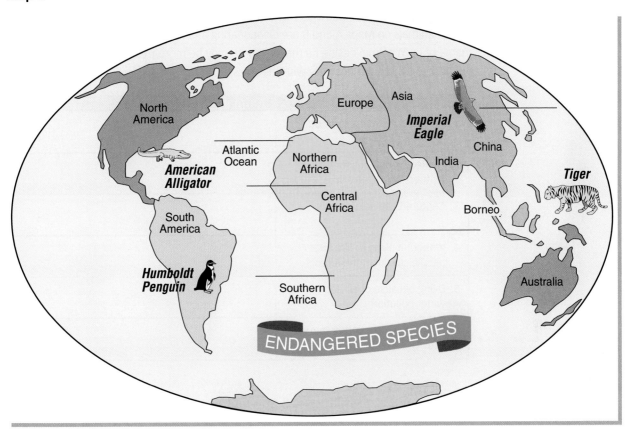

North America

Europe   Asia

Imperial Eagle

Atlantic Ocean

Northern Africa

China

India

American Alligator

Central Africa

Tiger

South America

Borneo

Humboldt Penguin

Southern Africa

Australia

ENDANGERED SPECIES

3 **Discussing Endangered Species** There are many reasons why animals are endangered. The chart below shows some of the reasons. Work in small groups. Decide which animals on Maps A and B are disappearing and for which reasons. Write the name of each animal beside its reason. There may be more than one reason for some animals. Discuss your answers with the class.

Reasons	Animals
1. Hunted by humans for food	
2. Hunted by humans for furs, feathers, tusks, etc.	
3. Captured and sold as pets	
4. Without a place to live after people cut down the forests	
5. Dying because of air and water pollution	
6. Dying because of other human activity	

4 **Researching Endangered Species** Visit the World Wildlife Organization at www.worldwildlife.org. Answer the questions.

1. Search by area of the world. What species are endangered in your area?

2. Find information to fill out the following chart. Report your results to the class.

Animal	Reason for Endangerment	What People are Doing to Solve the Problem

Self-Assessment Log

Check the words and expressions that you learned in this chapter.

Nouns
- ❏ campus
- ❏ carbon dioxide
- ❏ endangered species
- ❏ environment
- ❏ exhibit
- ❏ faucet
- ❏ pollution
- ❏ recyclables
- ❏ shuttle bus
- ❏ student union
- ❏ topsoil
- ❏ toxic chemicals

Verbs
- ❏ give a speech
- ❏ plant
- ❏ pollute
- ❏ recycle
- ❏ support

Adjectives
- ❏ mature
- ❏ slaughtered
- ❏ veggie (vegetable or vegetarian)

Expression
- ❏ a lot going on

Check the things you did in this chapter. How well can you do each one?

	Very well	Fairly well	Not very well
I can listen for the main ideas.	❏	❏	❏
I can listen for specific information.	❏	❏	❏
I can guess the meanings of words from context.	❏	❏	❏
I can identify stress and reductions.	❏	❏	❏
I can listen for emphasis to understand meaning.	❏	❏	❏
I can use expressions to tell my opinion.	❏	❏	❏
I can participate in a debate.	❏	❏	❏
I can use the Internet to find current news.	❏	❏	❏
I can talk about the environment and endangered species.	❏	❏	❏

Write about what you learned and what you did in this chapter.

In this chapter,

I learned _____

_____

I liked _____

_____

Audioscript

Chapter 1 Neighborhoods, Cities, and Towns

Part 1 Conversation: Hometowns

4 Listening for Main Ideas page 6

5 Listening for Specific Information page 6

7 Listening for Stressed Words page 7

Ali: Beth! Hey, Beth! How's it going?

Beth: Ali! Hi! I'm fine. How're you?

Ali: Fine, thanks. Beth, this is Lee. Lee, this is my friend, Beth.

Lee: Nice to meet you.

Beth: Nice to meet you. Are you from around here?

Lee: No, I'm from Seoul, Korea.

Beth: Really? That's interesting. Seoul's the capital of Korea, isn't it?

Lee: Yes, that's right. How about you? What's your hometown?

Beth: I'm from San Anselmo, California.

Lee: San An-sel-mo? Is that a big city?

Beth: No, it's a small town in Northern California. There are about 20,000 people there. What's the population of Seoul?

Lee: It's a really big city. There are over ten million people in Seoul.

Beth: Wow! That's a lot of people!

Lee: Yes, it is. But there's good public transportation, so it isn't bad.

Beth: How about the nightlife? Are there any good clubs or discos?

Lee: Are you kidding? There are hundreds! Seoul has fantastic nightlife!

Beth: [Pause] . . . Uh-oh. I have to run. The library closes in ten minutes. See you guys later.

Lee: Bye, Beth.

Ali: Take care, Beth.

Beth: You too. Bye.

8 Comparing Long Forms and Contractions page 8

Long Form

1. How is it going?
2. I am fine.
3. Seoul is the capital.
4. It is a really big city.
5. That is a lot of people!
6. There is good public transportation.

Contraction

1. How's it going?
2. I'm fine.
3. Seoul's the capital.
4. It's a really big city.
5. That's a lot of people!
6. There's good public transportation.

9 Listening for Contractions page 8

1. I'm fine.
2. He is from Seoul.
3. It's the capital of Korea.
4. There is great nightlife there.
5. What's the population?

Part 2   Using Language

1 Listening for Personal Information
page 13

Narrator: Conversation 1.

Ms. Dunn: What is your name?

Gordon McKay: Gordon McKay. That's G-O-R-D-O-N M-C-K-A-Y.

Ms. Dunn: And what is your address?

Gordon McKay: I live at 1223 East Park Avenue, Apartment 2B.

Ms. Dunn: That's 1223 East Park, Apartment 2B?

Gordon McKay: That's right.

Ms. Dunn: What is your telephone number?

Gordon McKay: My number is 555-7950.

Ms. Dunn: 555-7950?

Gordon McKay: That's right.

Ms. Dunn: Thank you.

Narrator: Conversation 2.

Ms. Dunn: What is your name?

Alicia Morales: Alicia Morales. A-L-I-C-I-A M-O-R-A-L-E-S.

Ms. Dunn: And where do you live?

Alicia Morales: I live at 456 Southern Avenue.

Ms. Dunn: What is your telephone number?

Alicia Morales: 555-2486.

Ms. Dunn: 555-2486?

Alicia Morales: Yes.

Ms. Dunn: And do you have a fax number?

Alicia Morales: Yes. It's 555-2489.

Ms. Dunn: Thank you.

Narrator: Conversation 3.

Ms. Dunn: Your name, please?

Sherry Wu: My name is Sherry Wu.

Ms. Dunn: Is that W-O-O?

Sherry Wu: No, it's W-U.

Ms. Dunn: And how do you spell your first name?

Sherry Wu: It's S-H-E-R-R-Y.

Ms. Dunn: And your address?

Sherry Wu: It's P.O. Box 45678, Shing Wong Street, Hong Kong.

Ms. Dunn: Phone number?

Sherry Wu: 2555-1234

Ms. Dunn: Do you have an email address?

Sherry Wu: Yes. It's swu@freemail.net.

Ms. Dunn: Okay. Thank you.

Narrator: Conversation 4.

Unpleasant guy: Hey there, what's your name?

Lisa: Uhh . . . Lisa.

Unpleasant guy: Uh, Lisa what?

Lisa: I'd rather not say.

Unpleasant guy: So what's your phone number, Lisa?

Lisa: Sorry, I don't give out personal information.

Part 3   Listening

2 Using Context Clues page 15

Narrator: Conversation 1.

Beth: Alicia, this is my friend Jamie.

Alicia: Pleased to meet you.

Jamie: Nice to meet you. Are you from around here?

Alicia: No, I'm from Mexico.

Jamie: Where in Mexico—Mexico City?

Alicia: Uh-huh.

Jamie: So, what's the city like?

Alicia: It's huge. There're around twenty million people living there.

Narrator: **Question 1.** What is Mexico City like?

Jamie: Wow! That's a really big city!

Alicia: Yeah, it sure is. I think it's the largest city in the world.

Narrator: Conversation 2.

Ali: So, Lee. Are you going home for New Year's?

Lee: Are you kidding? Seoul's pretty far from here!

Ali: That's no problem. There're a lot of flights to Seoul from this city.

Lee: Yeah, but you're forgetting one important thing.

Ali: What's that?

Lee: The airfare! I'm a student, and I only work part-time, remember?

Narrator: **Question 2.** Why isn't Lee going home for New Year's?

Ali: So, how much is it to Seoul?

Lee: Almost a thousand dollars! That's too much money for me!

Narrator: Conversation 3.

Man: Excuse me, driver. Does this bus go to Central Avenue?

Bus Driver: Yes, it's the second stop.

Man: So it's not very far?

Bus Driver: Nah! It's only about a half a mile.

Man: Really! Well, it's a nice day today, and I'm not in a hurry. And if it's that close . . . hmm . . .

Narrator: **Question 3.** How will the man go to Central Avenue?

Bus Driver: C'mon, buddy! Are you getting on the bus or not?

Man: Sorry, driver. I'll just walk to Central Avenue. Thanks anyway.

Narrator: Conversation 4.

Beth: So, how do you get to the university every day?

Lee: I take the subway. It's really fast from my apartment. How 'bout you?

Beth: Yeah, the subway is fast . . . but I take the bus instead.

Lee: Why? It's so slow . . .

Beth: Well, I can always get a seat. And there's room for all my books.

Narrator: **Question 4.** Why doesn't Beth take the subway?

Lee: Yeah, I know what you mean. The subway is way too crowded . . .

Beth: Yeah, the bus is much more comfortable.

Narrator: Conversation 5.

Ali: Hey, Lee. How's it goin'?

Lee: Great. What's new with you?

Ali: I've got a new place to live.

Lee: Hey, that's great. What's it like?

Ali: Well, it's really old and it's pretty small . . . but the best thing is it's a five-minute walk to school!

Narrator: **Question 5.** What does Ali like about his new place to live?

Lee: Wow, you're really close to school!

Ali: Yeah, that way, I can sleep longer in the morning!

5 **Listening for Main Ideas** page 17

6 **Listening for Specific Information** page 17

Woman: So, how do you get to school every day?

Man: I take the subway. It's fast.

Woman: You don't take the bus?

Man: Nah, the bus is too slow. It takes thirty minutes to get to school from my place.

Woman: Yeah, I know what you mean.

Man: How 'bout you?

Woman: Oh, I walk. My apartment's close. About one mile from school. It's just a fifteen-minute walk.

Man: Wow, that's great. My place is far from school—about ten miles. So I can't walk . . .

Woman: Yeah, that's about a three-hour walk!

10 **Listening for Main Ideas** page 19

11 **Listening for Specific Information** **(Part 1)** page 19

12 **Listening for Specific Information** **(Part 2)** page 19

Public Transportation in Vancouver, Canada

There are many kinds of public transportation in Vancouver. There are buses, ferries, the Sky Train elevated railway, and the West Coast Express trains. The transportation system is divided into three zones for the buses, ferries, and Sky Train. The regular fares are $2.25 for one zone, and $3.25 for two zones, and $4.50 for three zones. In the evening, on weekends, and on holidays, the fare is $2.25 for all zones. There are special fares for seniors, students, and children: $1.50 for one zone, $2.00 for two zones, and $3.00 for three zones. You need exact change for tickets on the bus. For the ferry and the Sky Train, you buy tickets in advance at machines at the station. To save money, buy a day pass. It's good for travel all day long on any form of transportation. A day pass costs $8.00 for adults and $6.00 for children.

Chapter 2 Shopping and E-Commerce

Part 1 Conversation: Shopping

5 Listening for Main Ideas (Part 1)
page 30

6 Listening for Main Ideas (Part 2)
page 31

7 Listening for Specific Information
page 31

10 Listening for Stressed Words page 33

Alicia: Hi, Beth. Come on in.

Beth: Hi, Alicia! How are you doing?

Alicia: Pretty good.

Beth: Alicia, this is my friend Ali. He's from Silver Spring, Maryland.

Alicia: Hi, Ali. It's nice to meet you.

Ali: Nice to meet you, too.

Alicia: Well, please come in and have a seat.

Beth, Ali: Thanks!

Alicia: Can I get you something? Coffee? Soda?

Beth: Oh, no thanks.

Ali: No thank you. I'm fine.

Beth: So, Alicia, we're going to go shopping. Do you want to come?

Alicia: Gee, I don't know . . . I shop mostly online these days.

Ali: Really? Why is that?

Alicia: Because it saves time—and gas!

Ali: Oh, right!

Beth: What do you mean?

Ali: Well, you don't have to drive your car . . .

Alicia: Right. And you don't have to look for parking. The mall is so crowded these days.

Beth: Yeah, but online you can't see things very well. And you can't touch them! And, with clothes, you can't try them on! I like to browse when I go shopping!

Ali: Me, too! . . . and it's such a nice day . . . why do you want to sit in front of a computer screen?

Alicia: Yeah, I see what you mean . . . but I don't have much money!

Beth: No problem! You can come with us and save money.

Alicia: How?

Beth: We aren't going to take any money or credit cards with us. And we aren't going to spend any money. We're just going to look around.

Ali: That's right! We're going *window*-shopping.

Alicia: Great idea! Then I *am* going!

12 Listening for Reductions page 34

1. b. It's nice to meetchya.*

2. b. Arencha* comin'?

3. a. I'm spending too much money.

4. a. Do you want to go shopping?

5. b. Do you hafta* study today?

Part 2 Using Language

1 Listening for Reasons page 37

2 Listening for Specific Information
page 38

Clerk: May I help you?

Customer: Yes. I'd like to return this sweater.

Clerk: OK. Why are you returning the sweater?

Customer: Because it's not the right size.

Clerk: Do you have your receipt?

Customer: Yes. Here it is.

Clerk: OK. I need your name, please.

Customer: My name is Anna McGuire.

Clerk: And your address?

Customer: It's 452 West Hammond Street.

Clerk: OK. Here you go: $43.95.

Customer: Thank you!

Part 3 Listening

1 Using Context Clues page 39

Narrator: Conversation 1.

Beth: Wow! This is a really big mall!

Alicia: Yeah, it is. Hey, I think I want to spend some money after all!

Ali: Well, maybe there's a bank here.

Beth: No, she doesn't need a bank. She can just use that machine over there.

Alicia: Oh, yeah . . . Let's see if I have my card.

Ali: How much are you gonna take out?

Alicia: Oh, maybe $200.

Narrator: **Question 1.** What are Ali, Alicia, and Beth talking about?

Ali: So, what's that called—a change machine?

Alicia: No, it's an automated teller, right?

Beth: Yeah. Or ATM for Automated Teller Machine.

Ali: Wait a minute, have you forgotten? We aren't going to need that. We're saving our money, right? Let's just keep window-shopping.

Narrator: Conversation 2.

Ali: Hey! Let's go in here! Look at all that great equipment!

Beth: Uh-oh, Alicia! Ali loves soccer and baseball. He's going to want to do more than window-shopping in this store.

Alicia: I think you're right. C'mon, Ali. You're not going in there, are you?

Narrator: **Question 2.** What shop are Ali, Alicia, and Beth standing in front of now?

Ali: C'mon, just for a minute. I really love sports.

Alicia: Yes, but we're supposed to be window-shopping. Besides, mmm! Can you smell that?

Ali and Beth: Yeah!

Narrator: Conversation 3.

Beth: Fresh chocolate chip cookies!

Alicia: And brownies!

Ali: It all smells delicious. But we don't have any money, remember?

Alicia: Well, I do have about $4.00.

Ali: OK, let's go in!

Narrator: **Question 3.** Where are they going now?

Beth: Wow! What a great bakery! I'll have one chocolate chip cookie.

Alicia: They're $1.50 each, three for $4.00. We have just enough.

Ali: Thanks, Alicia. Mmm!

Narrator: Conversation 4.

Ali: Where to now?

Beth: How about across the way? We can spend a few minutes looking at the new magazines and best sellers.

Alicia: Well, if you really want to. But I don't really like English magazines.

Ali: I'll bet they have Spanish magazines.

Narrator: **Question 4.** Where are Ali and Beth going to go next?

Alicia: Nah, you two go to the bookstore. I'm going somewhere else.

Narrator: Conversation 5.

Beth: All right, Alicia. Then let's meet in front of the elevators in half an hour—at one o'clock, OK?

Alicia: OK. I'm going to look at some sweaters and boots. It's getting cold, you know.

Ali and Beth: OK.

Narrator: **Question 5.** Where is Alicia going?

Alicia: Oh, Beth. Isn't there a good clothing store on the first floor?

Beth: Yes, there is. Go down those stairs and turn right.

Ad 1

Are you looking for a great pair of jeans? How about Wild West jeans? Cost Club has Wild West blue jeans for only $29.99 a pair—the lowest price in town!

Ad 2

Get the best price on Wild West blue jeans at Larson's Discount House. Larson's has your favorite jeans for only $31.99. That's right . . . only $31.99! Hurry, before . . . [fade]

Ad 3

Morton's Department Store is having its Big Spring Sale! All your favorite brands are on sale now. Just listen to these prices: Wild West jeans for only $35.99! Spring Step . . . [fade]

SuperMall22.com

Online shoppers now have a special place to buy everything they need: SuperMall22.com. SuperMall22.com is a shopping website, but it's different from other online shopping sites. First of all, you can buy *anything* at SuperMall22.com. No more going to one site for food, another for gifts, and another for furniture. SuperMall22.com offers everything from groceries to clothes to refrigerators, all at one website, and all in one transaction. And no more filling out several different online forms with your credit card and shipping information. Another big difference is that SuperMall22.com promises to deliver your purchases *one day* after you place your order. Now that's really saving time . . .

Chapter 3 Friends and Family

Part 1 Conversation: Staying in Touch

Beth: Lee? Are you okay? What's the matter?

Ali: Yeah, Lee! Why are you so sad?

Lee: I'm reading an email from my mom in Korea.

Beth: Is she all right?

Lee: Yes, she's fine, but I miss her, and I miss my other family and friends in Korea. I guess I'm homesick.

Ali: Yeah, I sometimes get homesick for my family.

Beth: Me too. I really want to see my family and friends in California soon.

Ali: How often do you hear from your family, Lee?

Lee: Besides email, I get two or three letters a month. How about you?

Beth: I usually call home.

Ali: I usually stay in touch just by phone because it's easy.

Lee: Well, I really want to talk to my family. Email just isn't the same. But it's expensive to call Korea.

Beth: Oh, call them, Lee! Just talk for three minutes.

Ali: Yeah, that's not very expensive. In fact, you can use my phone card.

Beth: Good idea! Call now before we go to the movies. There's a pay phone over there.

Lee: You're right. I really need to talk to them. But wait for me, OK?

Beth: Great!

11 Listening for Reductions page 57

1. Are you OK?

2. I don't miss them very much.

3. I wanna* go to the movies with you.

4. What're* you doing?

5. Why're* you sad?

Part 2 Using Language

2 Listening for Conversation Starters
page 60

3 Listening for Details page 60

Susan: Excuse me. I don't think we've met. My name is Susan.

Juan: Nice to meet you, Susan. My name is Juan.

Susan: Nice to meet you, Juan. Where are you from?

Juan: I'm from the Dominican Republic. What about you?

Susan: I'm from Chicago. How do you like going to school here?

Juan: I like it a lot, but I miss my home and my family.

Susan: Yeah, I know what you mean. Well, I'm going to get something to eat now. Nice talking to you.

Juan: I've enjoyed talking to you too. I hope to see you again.

Susan: Yes. That would be nice.

Part 3 Listening

1 Using Context Clues page 63

Narrator: Conversation 1.

Peter: Where are you from, Beth?

Beth: I'm from California.

Peter: I've been there. It's nice.

Beth: Yeah, I sure miss it!

Narrator: **Question 1.** What is Beth homesick for?

Peter: It sounds like you're homesick for California.

Beth: That's right! But I'm going to visit there next year.

Narrator: Conversation 2.

John: Hello?

Beth: Hello, John? This is Beth.

John: Hi, Beth. How are you doing?

Beth: Fine, thanks. Is Dan home?

John: No, he's skiing. He isn't coming back until tomorrow night.

Beth: Hmm. OK. Would you tell him I called?

John: Sure.

Beth: Also, would you ask him to call me when he gets back?

John: OK, Beth. I will.

Narrator: **Question 2.** Who does Beth want to call her?

John: I'll have Dan call you tomorrow evening.

Beth: Thanks a lot, John. Bye.

John: Bye, Beth.

Narrator: Conversation 3.

Lee: Hi, Alicia! What are you doing?

Alicia: Hi, Lee. Oh, I'm looking at some pictures of my family.

Lee: Can I see them too?

Alicia: Of course. This is a picture of all of us. That's my mom and dad on the left.

Lee: Your mom's very pretty.

Alicia: Thanks . . . And that's my older brother next to Mom. My little sister is the one on the right. She's still in high school.

Narrator: **Question 3.** How many children are in Alicia's family?

Lee: So your parents had three children?

Alicia: Uh-huh. I'm the middle child.

Narrator: Conversation 4.

Ali: Hey, listen to this: My little brother started school last week!

Dan: Great. What else does it say?

Ali: My cousin Nabil got a new job, and his wife just had a baby.

Dan: Gee, it's great to get mail from home, isn't it?

Narrator: **Question 4.** What's Ali doing?

Ali: Yeah. After reading this letter from my parents, I don't feel so homesick anymore.

Narrator: Conversation 5.

Beth: I'm going to call my family, Ali. Can you wait for me?

Ali: Sure, but . . . er . . . Beth, y'know, it's not 5 P.M., and it's a weekday.

Beth: So?

Ali: Well, the rates are high now. They go down after five o'clock. It's 4:40 now. Let's wait a few minutes.

Beth: Hmm.

Ali: And if you want cheaper rates, wait until tomorrow. The rates are lower on Saturday and Sunday.

Narrator: **Question 5.** When can Beth get the cheapest rates?

Beth: All right. That's a good suggestion, Ali. I'll wait and call this weekend, on Saturday.

4 **Listening for the Main Idea** page 64

5 **Listening to Voice Mail** page 64

Outgoing ["Dan"]

Hello. This is Dan. I'm not in right now, but if you leave a message, I'll call you back as soon as I can.

Message 1

Hi, Dan. This is Amy. I'm sorry I couldn't meet you to go over your project today. I'm sick. Call me back . . . I'll be home all night. The number is 555-0135. Bye.

Message 2

Hello. This is Beth. I'm calling to find out if you want to go out to dinner with me tonight. I want to go to that new restaurant on 3rd street. Call me back at 555-0167, or meet me there at six o'clock.

Message 3

Hey, Dan. This is Peter. I need to borrow that English book from you . . . remember, the book we talked about? I'll come by your apartment about seven to pick it up. See you later.

Message 4

Hello, son. We're just calling to remind you that we're arriving tomorrow at 10:25 in the morning. You'll meet us at the airport, right? We're really looking forward to seeing you. Your mother can't wait. See you tomorrow.

9 **Listening for the Main Idea** page 66

10 **Listening to Descriptions of People**
page 66

Beth: OK, Lee, my friend Sue will sell you her old answering machine.

Lee: Great! How can I get it?

Beth: She's at the apartment. You'll recognize her: She's tall and slim, and she has short red hair.

Chapter 4 Health Care

Part 1 Conversation: Calling a Hospital

4 **Listening for Main Ideas (Part 1)**
page 74

5 **Listening for Main Ideas (Part 2)**
page 74

6 **Listening for Specific Information**
page 75

8 Listening for Stressed Words page 76

Recording: Welcome to Faber Hospital and clinics. If this is an emergency, please hang up and call 9-1-1. Please listen carefully as our menu options have changed. For the 24-hour pharmacy, please press 1. For Family Medicine, press 2. For the health clinic, press 3. To speak to the operator, please press 0 or just stay on the line.

Ali (thinking): Hmm. I need the clinic; I'll press 3.

Receptionist: Health clinic. Can I help you?

Ali: Yes. I think I have the flu. I feel awful.

Receptionist: Would you like to make an appointment?

Ali: Yes, I'd like to see a doctor.

Receptionist: All right. Could you come in tomorrow afternoon at one o'clock?

Ali: Yes, I can come then. Oh! Should I bring any money?

Receptionist: No—just your ID and insurance card.

Ali: OK.

Receptionist: Now, could I have your name and insurance number?

Ali: Yes. My family name is Halal, H-A-L-A-L. My first name is Ali, A-L-I. And my insurance number is 000-481-624.

Receptionist: OK. You're all set. Don't forget to bring your health insurance card when you come in tomorrow.

Ali: OK.

Receptionist: All right, we'll see you tomorrow at one.

Ali: Yes, thank-you . . . thank-you very much. Bye.

Receptionist: Bye.

10 Listening for Reductions page 77

1. C'n* I help you?

2. Would you like to make an appointment?

3. Cudja* come in tomorrow afternoon at one?

4. No—just your ID and insurance card.

Part 2 Using Language

2 Listening for Main Ideas page 80

3 Listening for Specific Information
page 80

Ramona: I had an argument with Sue. Now she won't talk to me. What should I do?

Rick: Well, Ramona, she's probably angry with you right now. Maybe that's why she doesn't want to talk to you.

Ramona: Yeah, you're right.

Rick: I think you should write her a very nice letter. Tell her that you still want to be friends.

Ramona: OK. Then what?

Rick: You should wait a week, and then call her again. Maybe then she'll talk to you.

Ramona: That's good advice. Thanks, Rick.

Part 3 Listening

2 Using Context Clues page 82

Narrator: Call 1.

Caller 1: Yes. I'd like to make an appointment.

Man: What seems to be the problem?

Caller 1: I've got a really bad headache.

Man: Did you take your temperature?

Caller 1: No, but I think I've got a fever. My head feels warm.

Man: Hmm. Sounds like the flu. When can you come in?

Narrator: **Question 1.** Who is the woman probably calling?

Man: Health clinic. May I help you?

Caller 1: Yes, I'd like to make an appointment.

Narrator: Call 2.

Caller 2: Hello. I'd like to report a stolen bicycle.

Man: May I have your name, please?

Caller 2: The last name is Chavez, C-H-A-V-E-Z. First name, Maria, M-A-R-I-A.

Man: Address?

Caller 2: 121 High Street, Apartment 3B.

Man: And where was the bike stolen from?

Caller 2: In front of my apartment building. It was . . .

Narrator: **Question 2.** Who is the woman probably calling?

Man: Police department. Officer Wyman speaking.

Caller 2: Hello. I'd like to report a stolen bicycle.

Narrator: Call 3.

Caller 3: Hi. My name's Beth Johnston. I'd like to make an appointment.

Man: All right, Beth. Is this for a checkup or a cleaning?

Caller 3: A checkup. I think I have a bad cavity. The side of my head hurts.

Man: Which tooth hurts?

Caller 3: One of the back ones.

Man: Let me see . . . We can see you this afternoon if you can come in at 4:30.

Narrator: **Question 3.** Who is the speaker calling?

Man: Dental clinic. This is Mr. Adams.

Caller 3: Hi. My name's Beth Johnston. I'd like to make an appointment.

Narrator: Call 4.

Caller 4: Please! You must help me! My apartment's on fire!

Woman: Please try to stay calm, sir. Where is the fire?

Caller 4: There's smoke everywhere!

Woman: Excuse me . . . are you out of the apartment?

Caller 4: Yes, I am! Please send help immediately!

Woman: Now, sir, stay calm. Where are you located?

Narrator: **Question 4.** Who is the man probably calling?

Woman: Fire department.

Caller 4: Please! You must help me! My apartment's on fire!

Narrator: Call 5.

Caller 5: Yes, I'd like to make an appointment.

Man: Have you ever been here before?

Caller 5: No, but I'm a student, and all of a sudden, I can't see things on the board in the front of the classroom very well . . .

Man: OK. It sounds like you need an exam.

Caller 5: Great. I've been so worried . . .

Narrator: **Question 5.** Who is the speaker calling?

Man: Eye clinic. This is Sean.

Caller 5: Yes, I'd like to make an appointment.

5 **Listening for the Main Idea** page 82

6 **Listening to Instructions** page 83

Ali: I feel like I have a very bad cold. I have a fever, I ache all over, and I cough and sneeze all the time.

Dr. Dirks: You probably have the flu, or influenza. It's much more serious than a cold. You have to take care of yourself, or you could become very sick. You should stay in bed and rest as much as possible. You can take two aspirin, four times a day. That will help the fever and the aches and pains. Be sure to drink plenty of fluids. Fruit juice and hot tea are the best. Here's a prescription for some cough medicine. You can take it to any drugstore. Be sure to take your medicine with your meals because it might upset your stomach.

Ali: I understand. Thanks.

Narrator: Number 1.

Speaker 1: I have a terrible headache. The pain is right at the back of my head. It seems to go from ear to ear.

Narrator: Number 2.

Speaker 2: I think I have the flu. I vomited twice after breakfast this morning. I guess I shouldn't eat anything.

Narrator: Number 3.

Speaker 3: I was playing soccer and fell over another player. Now I can't stand up or walk. I think I broke my leg.

Narrator: Number 4.

Speaker 4: I just had a drink with ice, and now my tooth really hurts—here on the right side of my mouth. I must have a cavity.

Narrator: Number 5.

Speaker 5: I tripped on the curb when crossing the street and twisted my ankle. I can walk, but it really hurts. I think I sprained it.

Narrator: Number 6.

Speaker 6: I don't feel too bad, but I kept sneezing and coughing in class today. I knew there was a cold going around, but I didn't think I would catch it.

Chapter 5 Men and Women

Part 1 Conversation: Going Out

Beth: OK, great! I'll see you tomorrow at seven o'clock. Right. Bye!

Alicia: Hmm. Who was that?

Lee: Yeah! Someone special?

Beth: That was Michel, a really nice guy in my computer science class. He asked me out. I accepted, so . . .

Alicia: So, one phone call, and now you have a boyfriend!

Beth: Oh, c'mon, Alicia. He's not my boyfriend—yet!

Alicia: Well, it sounds nice. I need my parents' permission to go out on a date with a boy.

Lee: Yeah . . . one of my friends here at the college is from India, and he says, in his country, parents used to arrange all dates—and marriages, too. *And sometimes they still do.*

Beth: Wow! That's interesting!

Alicia: Hmm! Lee! . . . you said your friend is from India?

Lee: That's right.

Alicia: And your friend is a guy, right?

Lee: Yes. His name is Varun.

Alicia: Well, a girlfriend of mine in my math class is from India, too! Her name is Parveena. Do you think Varun would like to meet her?

Lee: You mean on a date?

Beth: Sure. Why not? That's a great idea, Alicia.

Lee: I don't know. Maybe they need their parents' permission . . .

Alicia: Oh, come on, Lee!

Lee: OK, OK! I don't know why you want to be a matchmaker. But I'll ask Varun.

Alicia: Great! And I'll call Parveena!

10 Listening for Reductions page 97

1. What did you do last weekend?

2. Where ja* go on Sunday?

3. When did you get up this morning?

4. How ja* get to school?

5. Who ja* come to school with?

6. Why ja* take the bus?

Part 2 Using Language

2 Listening for Main Ideas page 99

3 Listening to Small Talk page 100

Woman: Hi. How are you?

Man: Fine. It's nice to see you. When did you get here?

Woman: Just a few minutes ago. I'm a little late because of the rain.

Man: Yes, it's been raining so much lately. I hope it'll stop soon.

Woman: I hope so. We're going to a baseball game tomorrow.

Man: Oh, are you a baseball fan? I saw the game last week. Our team's really good this year, isn't it?

Woman: Yes, I'm really looking forward to the game. Oh, I see Martha over there. Excuse me, I'm going to say hello to her.

Man: Of course. It was nice to see you. Have a good time tonight.

Part 3 Listening

2 Using Context Clues page 102

Narrator: Conversation 1.

Alicia: So, Beth, how was your date with that guy in your computer science class . . . what's his name?

Beth: Michel. We had a great time. Of course, on Friday night the Mann Theater is really crowded. We had to wait 45 minutes to get our tickets.

Alicia: Yeah, it's terrible on the weekend. But you finally got in?

Beth: Uh-huh. And after the movie, we went to Chez Hugo and had dinner.

Narrator: **Question 1.** What did Beth do on her date?

Alicia: So you went to a movie and then to a restaurant too, huh? That sounds nice!

Narrator: Conversation 2.

Jennifer: What happened to you? Do you know what time it is?

Rob: Jennifer, please try to understand. I tried to get here by one o'clock, but the traffic was terrible!

Jennifer: Rob, it's almost 2:30. The traffic couldn't be that bad.

Rob: I'm really sorry. It won't happen again.

Narrator: **Question 2.** Why is Jennifer upset?

Jennifer: Well, all right. But next time, call me if you're going to be late, OK?

Narrator: Conversation 3.

Dina: Hello?

Peter: May I speak to Dina, please?

Dina: This is Dina.

Pete: Hi, Dina. This is Peter.

Dina: Who?

Pete: Peter . . . from your chemistry class.

Dina: Oh, hi, Peter. What's up?

Pete: I called to see if you wanted to go with me to a movie. There's a good one at the Mann Theater this Friday night.

Dina: Oh, thanks, Peter, but I'm already doing something this Friday night.

Narrator: **Question 3.** What is Dina probably going to do?

Peter: Well, are you busy on Saturday? We can get a pizza or something.

Dina: Thanks, Peter, but I can't go out with you. I already have a boyfriend.

Narrator: Conversation 4.

Pat: Hello?

Peter: May I speak to Pat, please?

Pat: Speaking.

Peter: Hi, Pat. This is Peter from your English class.

Pat: Oh, hi, Peter. How're you doing?

Peter: Fine, thanks. Look, Pat, would you like to go to a movie with me on Friday night?

Pat: Oh, I'd like to, Peter, but I'm already doing something on Friday.

Narrator: **Question 4.** What is Pat probably going to do?

Peter: Oh, well. Maybe some other time.

Pat: Hey, I'm not doing anything on Saturday. How 'bout going to the concert in the park that evening?

Peter: Great idea! I'll pick you up at seven o'clock.

Narrator: Conversation 5.

Susan: Hey, Anu. Do you want to go to the concert on Saturday?

Anu: Uhh, yeah, sure. It's free, isn't it?

Susan: No, actually student tickets are $10 or $15 each, I think.

Anu: Hmm. Look, Susan, I'd like to go to the concert, but I don't think I can . . .

Narrator: **Question 5.** Why can't Anu go to the concert?

Susan: Why can't you go?

Anu: Well, I just don't think I have enough money to pay for you and me.

Susan: That's OK. I'm inviting you, so I'll pay.

6 Listening for Main Ideas page 104

7 Listening for Specific Information
page 104

Michel: Hello?

Beth: Hi, Michel. This is Beth. How are you?

Michel: Fine. How are you doing?

Beth: Great! I'm just calling to invite you over tomorrow night. My roommate and I are having a few people over for dinner. We might rent a movie. Can you come?

Michel: Sure. I'd love to come. What time?

Beth: About seven. It's going to be very informal.

Michel: Should I bring anything?

Beth: No, we have everything we need.

Michel: OK. Then I'll see you tomorrow around seven o'clock.

Beth: Great! See you then.

11 Listening for Main Ideas page 106

12 Listening for Specific Information
page 107

Dan: Hey, there's a basketball game on Friday night!

Ali: So?

Beth: Who's playing?

Dan: The Seals and the Bears.

Beth: That sounds exciting!

Dan: So, do you want to go with me?

Ali: Uh-h-h, gee, Dan, maybe some other time.

Dan: How about you, Beth?

Beth: I'd love to! I'll meet you at six o'clock.

Chapter 6 Sleep and Dreams

Part 1 Conversation: Sleep Deprived!

4 Listening for Main Ideas (Part 1)
page 114

5 Listening for Main Ideas (Part 2)
page 114

6 Listening for Specific Information
page 115

8 Listening for Stressed Words page 116

Beth: Ali! What's the matter? You look so sleepy!

Alicia: Yeah! Can't you wake up this morning?

Ali: No, I can't! I can hardly keep my eyes open! I was up late last night. My friend had a party. I only got about four hours of sleep.

Alicia: Why didn't you sleep in this morning?

Ali: I have to meet my study group at the library. We have a big test next week.

Beth: A big test? Why didn't you study last night instead of going to the party?

Ali: Oh, it's OK. I studied a lot before the party.

Alicia: Maybe that's not a good idea.

Ali: Why not?

Alicia: I read a research study. It said that if you don't get enough sleep after you study, you may forget 30 percent of what you studied! Especially if you studied something that is very complex.

Ali: Thirty percent? That's almost one-third!

Beth: Yes, that's a lot. Are you sure, Alicia?

Alicia: Yes. Even two days after you study—if you don't get enough sleep, you forget a lot. It's called being "sleep deprived."

Beth: Well, I read that eating right can help you study.

Ali: You mean what you eat helps you study?

Beth: Yes, there are chemicals that help you stay alert. I think the best foods are fish, eggs, soy, rice, and peanuts. So you should get enough sleep and eat the right foods.

Ali: That sounds like good advice! I'll see you two later!

Alicia: Where are you going, Ali?

Ali: Home to take a nap!

10 Distinguishing Between Teens and Tens page 117

1. He is <u>forty</u> years old.

2. I bought <u>thirteen</u> new books.

3. The price is <u>seventeen</u> dollars.

4. It happened in <u>1918</u>.

5. We stayed for <u>fifty</u> days.

6. I live at <u>60</u> New Hope Road.

Part 2   Using Language

2 Listening for Main Ideas page 121

3 Listening for Specific Information page 121

Lee: Alicia, how many hours a night do you sleep?

Alicia: Usually nine or ten.

Lee: Wow! That's a lot!

Alicia: I don't think so. I think people need different amounts of sleep.

Lee: Maybe you're right, but I read that eight hours is normal for most people.

Alicia: Perhaps that's the average, but don't you think that everyone is different?

Lee: I'm not sure. Eight hours seems like plenty to me.

Alicia: How many hours do you sleep?

Lee: Usually five or six.

Alicia: Five or six! No wonder you think nine is too much!

Part 3   Listening

1 Using Context Clues page 123

Narrator: Part 1.

Good morning, class. I hope you all had enough sleep last night. If you read the chapter, you know that the topic for today is Sleep and the Human Brain. First, I will review the importance of sleep. Then I will tell you about some new research on sleep and studying. Finally, I will discuss the health benefits of sleep.

Narrator: **Question 1.** What are you listening to?

This lecture will cover some of the information in your textbook and add some new information.

Narrator: Part 2.

We don't know why the human brain needs sleep. We do know that sleep is important for physical health and mental health. Your body needs sleep to stay healthy and strong. Your brain seems to need sleep for the same reason.

Narrator: **Question 2.** What does sleep do for your brain?

Sleep helps your brain stay healthy. It helps you think clearly and remember more.

Narrator: Part 3.

Carlyle Smith, a psychology professor in Canada, did some research on sleep. He studied how sleep affects memory. He started by teaching students two things: first, a list of words, and second, a difficult problem.

Narrator: **Question 3.** Why did Carlyle Smith teach the students a list of words and a difficult problem?

Then Smith tested the students to see how much they remembered of the list of words and the problem.

Narrator: Part 4.

Before he gave the students the test, he asked the students to sleep different amounts for the next three nights. Some students slept eight hours every night. Some students slept only four hours the first night; then they slept eight hours the next two nights. Some students slept eight hours the first night, only four hours the second night, and eight hours the third night. Some students slept eight hours the first night and eight hours the second night, but only four hours the third night.

Narrator: **Question 4.** Why did Smith have the students sleep different amounts on the first, second, and third nights?

Smith wanted to see if sleeping only a few hours for three nights after learning something new affects the memory.

Narrator: Part 5.

The results of the research showed that people remember better when they get enough sleep. Of course, the students who slept eight hours every night did the best on the test. They remembered the list of words and the difficult problem very well. The students who slept only four hours the second night after learning the words and the problem also did very well. But the results were very different for the students who slept only four hours on the first night or the third night.

Narrator: **Question 5.** How did the students who didn't sleep much on the first or third nights remember the difficult problem?

Students who didn't sleep much on the first and third nights did not do well on the test or the difficult problem. They couldn't remember how to solve the problem. Smith concluded that it is very important to sleep enough the night after you learn something new <u>and</u> the third night after—but it might be safe to stay up late on the second night!

5 **Listening for Main Ideas** page 125

6 **Listening for Details** page 125

Carlyle Smith's study on memory and sleep showed some interesting results. There were four subject groups of students in the study. All the students learned a list of words and how to solve a complex problem. The first group of students slept eight hours a night for three nights after learning the new material. One week later, they took a test on the words and the problem. They remembered all the material. Most scored 100 percent on both tests—on the list of words and the complex problem.

The second subject group only slept four hours the night after learning the material—they were sleep-deprived the first night. One week later, they still remembered the list of words, but they didn't remember how to solve the complex problem. Most scored 100 percent on the list of words, but only 70 percent on the complex problem.

The third subject group was sleep-deprived the second night after learning the new material. Strangely, they scored just as well as the first group. Most answered 98 percent of the questions correctly on both tests—the list of words and the complex problem.

The fourth group slept well the first and second night, but they were sleep-deprived on the third night. This group had the same memory problems as the group that was sleep-deprived on the first night. They remembered the list of words, but not how to solve the problem. Their scores on the tests were the same as the second group.

11 **Listening for Main Ideas** page 127

I had the strangest dream last night! I was going to the movies with Beth. I went to her apartment to get her. When I arrived, Beth was wearing normal clothes. But I wasn't wearing normal clothes; I was wearing a bathing suit, flippers, and a face mask. Beth said, "Ali, take off that face mask! I can't see your face." I tried to take the face mask off, but I couldn't take it off. Then I tried to take the flippers off, but my arms couldn't move. Beth tried to help me take the mask off, but she couldn't take it off either. Then, she tried to help me take off my flippers. She pulled on a flipper and I fell backwards and I broke a vase. I was so embarrassed!

Chapter 7 Work and Lifestyles

Part 1 Conversation: Looking for a Summer Job

Alicia: Thanks for coming with me to the Placement Center, Ali.

Ali: Don't mention it. It's nice to have your company. Besides, I need to find a summer job, too!

Alicia: What kind of job are you looking for, Ali?

Ali: I'm hoping to find one in my major, public health.

Alicia: I'm sure you can. Do you have any experience in public health?

Ali: Yes, I do. I worked part-time in a lab in Maryland last summer.

Alicia: That's great. I want to find a job writing for a local newspaper. I'd like to be a reporter.

Ali: Your major's journalism, isn't it?

Alicia: Uh-huh. I had a great job last summer when I was in Mexico City.

Ali: Really? What did you do?

Alicia: I worked part-time for *Excelsior*. It's the biggest newspaper in Mexico.

Ali: What did you do there?

Alicia: I wrote local news stories—you know, news about Mexico City. But someday I want to write international news stories. Then I can travel around the world and find out what people are like in other places.

Ali: That sounds wonderful. I'm sure you can do it.

Alicia: Are there any jobs in public health on the bulletin board?

Ali: No, I don't see anything interesting.

Alicia: You should try looking on the Web. There are some great job sites. That's how I found the job in Mexico City.

Ali: That's a good idea. Do I search for "public health"?

Alicia: Try "jobs in public health" or the names of specific jobs. I searched for "newspaper reporter."

Ali: I'll go to the computer lab right now and try that! See you later.

1. He's a journalist.

2. I study economics.

3. Elizabeth is a psychologist.

4. Are you an accountant?

5. I majored in biology.

6. She's a physicist.

7. Do you study technology?

Part 2   Using Language

Ann: Uh-h-h, Paula, may I speak to you for a minute?

Paula: Sure, Ann. What is it?

Ann: I'm having a problem with one of the other account managers. She's always late for work, so I have to do her work too.

Paula: Did you discuss this with her?

Ann: I talked to her last week, but she is still coming late every day. I had to make a presentation to a client for her this morning.

Paula: Well, let's talk to her together and see if we can come up with a solution. Meet me in my office at 3:00.

Ann: Thanks, Paula.

Part 3   Listening

Narrator: Conversation 1

Interviewer: Come in!

Alicia: Excuse me. May I see you now? I have an appointment.

Interviewer: Of course. You're . . . Alicia?

Alicia: Yes, that's right. Alicia Morales.

Interviewer: And you're interested in working for us?

Alicia: Yes. I have some experience. I was a part-time reporter last summer for *Excelsior.*

Interviewer: I see. Well, this sample of your writing is excellent.

Narrator: **Question 1** Who is Alicia talking to?

Interviewer: As manager of our newspaper, I think we might have an opening in the international news department.

Alicia: Oh, I hope so! I would love to work on international stories!

Narrator: Conversation 2

Dan: What are you going to do this summer, Sang-mi? Going back to Korea?

Sang-mi: I'd like to, Dan, but I have to think about my future.

Dan: Your future? What do you mean?

Sang-mi: Well, someday I want to help sick people. So I want to get some hospital experience.

Dan: You mean working part-time in one?

Sang-mi: Uh-huh.

Narrator: **Question 2.** What does Sang-mi want to do this summer?

Dan: If you want to work in a hospital, you should visit County General Hospital. They may have part-time summer jobs.

Sang-mi: I will. Thanks.

Narrator: Conversation 3.

Sang-mi: So how about you, Dan? What are your summer plans?

Dan: I'm still not sure what I'm going to do. I should study, but my friend Bill—y'know, the one in San Francisco?

Sang-mi: Oh, right.

Dan: He wants me to go with him to Europe in July and August.

Sang-mi: Really?

Dan: Yeah. I'm thinking about it.

Narrator: **Question 3.** What is Dan thinking about doing this summer?

Sang-mi: That's a great plan. You *should* go to Europe this summer.

Narrator: Conversation 4.

Dan: Yes, but I have to think about September.

Sang-mi: Aren't you going to go back to school?

Dan: Well, I *should* go back. But I'm getting tired of school. I want more experience in the real world.

Sang-mi: So you want more job experience?

Dan: Uh-huh.

Narrator: **Question 4.** What does Dan want to do in the fall?

Sang-mi: I know how you feel. I want to work too, but I have to get out of school first.

Narrator: Conversation 5.

Dan: Is that because you're an international student?

Sang-mi: That's right. I can only study with my student visa, except in the summer. Then I can work part-time.

Narrator: **Question 5.** Can Sang-mi work?

Dan: So you can work only in the summer? That's rough.

Sang-mi: Oh, it's not bad. But I have to be careful with money!

5 **Listening for Main Ideas** page 145

6 **Listening for Specific Information** page 145

Claudia: Rafael, your résumé is very impressive. Please tell me why you're interested in this job.

Rafael: Well, I like working with computers, and the job sounds very challenging.

Claudia: I see. Why should I give you a job with this company?

Rafael: My work is accurate, and I learn quickly. In fact, I really like learning new information and new skills!

Claudia: Good. You'll have a lot to learn here. Tell me, Rafael, what do you think you'll be doing in ten years?

Rafael: I like working with people, so I'd like to be a department manager in ten years.

10 **Listening for the Main Idea** page 147

11 **Listening to Future Plans** page 148

Father: So what are your plans for this summer, Dan?

Dan: Well, I could work for that construction company again. But I have a great opportunity to do some traveling and learn more about the world.

Father: What's that?

Dan: My friend Bill is going to travel around

Europe this summer—he has some relatives in France he wants to visit, and he plans to go to Germany, Lithuania, and Latvia. He'll have a rental car, so all I need to pay for is my airfare and meals.

Father: What about hotels when you're not staying with Bill's relatives?

Dan: We'll stay in youth hostels. They're really cheap. I have enough money saved from my part-time job.

Father: What about money for next year? For your books and other expenses?

Dan: Well, I'll need to borrow a little from you. But this is a once in a lifetime chance. I really think I could learn a lot, and I can improve my French, too!

Chapter 8 Food and Nutrition

Part 1 Conversation: At a Food Court

4 **Listening for Main Ideas** page 155

5 **Listening for Specific Information** (Part 1) page 156

6 **Listening for Specific Information** (Part 2) page 156

8 **Listening for Stressed Words** page 157

Dan: Wow! Look at all these different places to eat!

Pat: You said it! There are so many choices: American "fast food," Chinese, Italian, vegetarian! I can't decide what to eat!

Meryl: What are you going to have, Dan?

Dan: I'm hungry! I'm going to the fast-food place. I want a double cheeseburger and a large order of fries.

Pat: Ugh! How many cheeseburgers do you eat

every week? You had a couple at the picnic yesterday, didn't you?

Dan: Yeah, . . . Yeah . . . so *what?* I *like* cheeseburgers!

Meryl: I think Pat's worried about you.

Dan: Why? I'm healthy!

Pat: But cheeseburgers have a lot of fat.

Meryl: And a lot of calories.

Dan: OK, OK! What are *you* going to have?

Pat: I'm going to have some tofu and rice at that Chinese place.

Dan: Oh, I forgot. You're a vegetarian, right?

Pat: Right.

Meryl: Hmm. I think I'm going to have a salad.

Dan: Are you on a diet?

Meryl: No diet—I just like to eat healthy food.

Dan: What are you going to have to drink?

Meryl: A large cola.

Dan: A large cola? But there's lots of sugar in soda!

Pat: Dan's right. And sugar's bad for your teeth.

Meryl: All right! I'll have a *diet* cola. There's no sugar in that!

Dan: Great! And *I'll* have a salad too.

10 **Listening for Reductions** page 158

1. What're* ya* gonna* have?

2. I think I'm gonna* have some tofu 'n rice.

3. We would like a couple of salads.

4. Isn't there a lotta* fat in cheeseburgers?

5. They don't want to eat lots of fatty food.

Part 2   Using Language

2 **Listening for the Main Idea** page 161

3 **Listening for Specific Information** page 162

4 **Ordering in a Restaurant** page 163

Narrator: Conversation 1

Maitre d': Two for dinner?

Alicia: Yes. We'd like to sit near the window, please.

Maitre d': Of course. Come right this way.

Narrator: Conversation 2

Waitress: Would you like to order something to drink while you look at the menu?

Alicia: Yes. I'd like hot tea, please.

Lee: I'll just have water.

Waitress: I'll bring your drinks and take your order in just a minute.

Narrator: Conversation 3

Waitress: Are you ready to order?

Alicia: Yes. I'll have the mushroom ravioli.

Waitress: A salad comes with that. What kind of dressing would you like—French, Italian, or ranch?

Alicia: French, please.

Lee: And I'd like the spaghetti with tomato sauce.

Waitress: What kind of dressing would you like on your salad—French, Italian, or ranch?

Lee: Italian dressing, please.

Narrator: Conversation 4

Waitress: Is everything all right here?

Alicia: Could I have some lemon for my tea, please?

Waitress: Certainly. Anything else?

Lee: No, everything's fine, thanks.

Narrator: Conversation 5

Waitress: Can I get you anything else tonight? Some dessert or coffee?

Alicia: No, thank you. Just the check, please.

Waitress: Here you are. I hope you enjoyed your dinner. Come back soon.

Part 3   Listening

2 **Using Context Clues** page 164

Narrator: Conversation 1

Lee: Everything looks delicious! What are you going to have?

Alicia: Dan says the onion soup here tastes great. I think that's what I'll have.

Lee: That sounds good.

Narrator: **Question 1.** Where are Lee and Alicia?

Lee: Y'know, it's really nice to eat in a restaurant.
Alicia: It sure is.

Narrator: Conversation 2
Waiter: Here you go. Was everything okay?
Alicia: Yes, thank you. Everything was delicious.
Lee: Yes, it was. But, excuse me.
Waiter: Yes?
Lee: What's this charge for?
Waiter: Hmm. Let me see. Oh, yes. That's for your drinks. One hot tea, $1.85 , and one cola, $2.25.

Narrator: **Question 2.** What's Lee asking about?

Lee: Oh, I see. Thanks for explaining the bill.
Waiter: You're welcome, sir.

Narrator: Conversation 3.
Beth: Now, Dan. What's next?
Dan: Hmm. Just a minute. Ah, . . . one cup of milk.
Beth: A cup of milk.
Dan: One teaspoon of salt.
Beth: A teaspoon of salt.
Dan: And one egg.
Beth: Right.
Dan: Beat the milk, salt, and egg mixture thoroughly and . . .

Narrator: **Question 3.** What are Dan and Beth doing?

Dan: This is fun, isn't it?
Beth: Yes, it is. I really enjoy cooking.
Dan: But eating is even better!

Narrator: Conversation 4.
Ali: Wow! This place is really big!
Alicia: It *is* big, isn't it?
Ali: Look at all this food!
Alicia: Here's what we need for the salad. What's on the list?

Ali: Let's see—lettuce, tomatoes, carrots, and cucumbers.

Narrator: **Question 4.** Where are Ali and Alicia?

Ali: All these fruits and vegetables look so fresh!
Alicia: Yeah. These big supermarkets have good produce!

Narrator: Conversation 5.
Ali: So, do we have everything on the shopping list?
Alicia: I think so. Oh! We need spaghetti sauce. It's over there . . .
Ali: Here it is. What kind should we buy?
Alicia: Hmm. Here's one . . . spaghetti sauce with mushrooms . . . eight ounces, $1.06.
Ali: That looks good. But here's another kind. It's only 99 cents.
Alicia: Really? Let me see the label . . . spaghetti sauce with mushrooms . . . oh, but look *here,* Ali. There's only *six* ounces in this one.

Narrator: **Question 5.** Which spaghetti sauce is the best price?

Ali: Oh, yeah, you're right. The eight-ounce size for $1.06 is the best price. Let's buy that one.

5 **Listening for Main Ideas** page 165

6 **Listening to Instructions** page 165

Ali: Beth, Alicia—I'm so happy to see you! I need some help.
Beth: What's the problem, Ali?
Ali: Well, you know I never cooked before I came to the university.
Alicia: Uh-huh.
Ali: I asked my mother for some recipes so I can make my favorite dishes. She sent me these, but I don't understand the instructions.
Beth: We can try to help, Ali. What are the instructions you don't understand?
Ali: First it says to "chop" some onions. How do I do that?
Alicia: "Chop" just means to cut them up into very small pieces with a knife.

Ali: Oh, OK. I get it. Now this one says to "brown" the onions.

Beth: That means to cook them in a little oil until they turn brown all over.

Ali: I've never seen *"brown"* as a verb before! This one, "mix thoroughly," I understand. It means to mix the things together completely, right?

Beth: Right.

Ali: What about this—"grate" the cheese? How do I grate cheese?

Alicia: You need a special tool for that—a cheese grater. It has little holes and sharp points on it so that when you rub the cheese over it, thin bits of the cheese fall through the holes. Then you can put the cheese on top of other foods like pizza. I have a cheese grater you can borrow.

Ali: Great! Thanks a lot. I'll invite you for dinner when I finish!

10 **Listening for the Main Idea** page 168

11 **Ordering Steps in a Recipe** page 168

Hi. I'm Wally Chan. Welcome to "Chan Cooks." Today I'm making chili. You make chili with beans, beef, and tomatoes.

First, you chop an onion. Cut it into small pieces. Then, brown the onion and some ground beef in a little oil. Cook the onion and beef in the oil until the onion is a little brown, and the beef is all brown. Now, add tomatoes and chili powder to the beef and onion. Chili powder is hot, so just use a little if you don't like spicy food. Cook this mixture for about an hour, stirring occasionally.

OK. Here's what it looks like when it's done. I like to serve the chili in a bowl with some shredded cheese on top. Enjoy!

12 **Discussing Opinions About Food**
page 169

1. I like onions on my hamburgers.

2. Chili powder makes food too hot and spicy.

3. I eat a lot of cheese—with crackers, bread, and other foods.

4. Tomatoes are best in salad, with lettuce, oil, and vinegar.

5. I like beans when they are cooked with onions and garlic.

6. Cooking with oil can make you fat.

7. The best pizza has just tomato sauce and lots of cheese.

8. Foods like beans, rice, and potatoes should be eaten at every meal.

9. Onions are good cooked and uncooked.

10. I like a lot of salt in my food.

Chapter 9 Great Destinations

Part 1   Conversation: Arriving in San Francisco

4 **Listening for Main Ideas (Part 1)**
page 178

5 **Listening for Main Ideas (Part 2)**
page 178

6 **Listening for Specific Information**
page 179

8 **Listening for Stressed Words** page 181

Beth: Look, guys, up ahead! There's San Francisco! We're almost there!

Ali: Look at that skyline! What's that tall, triangular building? It looks like a tower.

Dan: That's the Transamerica Building. It's one of San Francisco's landmarks. It's almost as famous now as the Golden Gate Bridge, the cable cars, Chinatown . . .

Ali: Well, I can't wait to go to all those places . . . and Alcatraz, too.

Beth: You said it! Alcatraz used to be the prison where the most dangerous criminals in the United States were put. Now, it's a really interesting *former* prison and great place to tour.

Dan: Let's try to go there tomorrow. Then, we can also do something else tomorrow . . . Uh-oh!

Beth: Dan! What's wrong with the car?

Ali: Yeah! Why are we going slower?

Dan: Oh, *no!* I think we have a flat tire!

Beth: We have a spare tire, don't we?

Dan: Yes, I think so. I'll pull over.

Dan: There it is. It *is* a flat tire. Now, who can help me change it?

Beth and Ali: I can!

Beth: I can't believe we have a flat tire . . . and just before we got to San Francisco!

Ali: Oh, it'll take us just a few minutes to change it. Then, we can start to explore the city!

Part 2   Using Language

2 Listening for Main Ideas page 184

3 Listening for Specific Information
page 185

Narrator: Conversation 1.

Lee: Ali, it's a perfect day to go to the beach. Let's go!

Ali: I think it's a little too cold to spend a day at the beach. I'd rather go on a bike ride. Come and ride to the Prospect Park Lake with me. We can stop for ice cream on the way back.

Lee: OK. That sounds good. I'll get my bike.

Narrator: Conversation 2.

Alicia: Hey, Beth. Do you want to go shopping at the mall today?

Beth: I think I've been spending too much money lately. Wouldn't you rather go for a nice walk in the mountains? It's free!

Alicia: You're right. We should get more exercise. Let me put on my walking shoes and we can go.

Narrator: Conversation 3.

Dan: Ming, should we go out to dinner tonight?

Ming: Sure, Dan. Where do you want to go?

Dan: Well, I have some menus here. There's a new Mexican restaurant on Poplar. Let's go there.

Ming: Oh, I ate there last night. It was a little too spicy for me. Couldn't we go to Wang's instead?

Dan: I guess so. Chinese is good, too. Let's go!

Part 3   Listening

2 Using Context Clues page 189

Narrator: Conversation 1.

Beth: Well, we've got everything in the trunk.

Dan: I thought the tent wasn't going to fit!

Ali: The sleeping bags and fishing equipment take up a lot of space, too.

Beth: You guys have too much luggage, too.

Narrator: **Question 1.** What did Beth, Dan, and Ali finish doing?

Beth: We just got everything in the car, and it's already almost lunchtime!

Narrator: Conversation 2.

Dan: Yes, so let's go find something to eat.

Beth: Where? There's not a town or restaurant anywhere *near* here.

Ali: Yes, there is. Look at this map. There's a town about five miles from here.

Dan: You're right! Let's go!

Narrator: **Question 2.** What are Beth, Dan, and Ali going to do?

Beth: I'm so glad there's a town near here. It must have a restaurant or two. I'm really hungry!

Narrator: Conversation 3.

Ali: Well, that was a great lunch.

Beth: Yeah, we were lucky to find such a good restaurant way out here.

Dan: Thanks to you and your map!

Ali: Nah, it was easy. Say, why is it so dark outside?

Beth: Look at that sky! I don't like this. It's really cloudy.

Dan: You're right. I'll turn on the radio.

Narrator: Question 3. Why is Dan going to turn on the radio?

Ali: Yes, see if you can find a weather report.

Narrator: Conversation 4.

Radio: . . . and in southern New Mexico, there's a flash flood advisory through this evening with a 50 percent chance of rain this afternoon, increasing to 70 percent tonight. Lows expected tonight near freezing.

Narrator: Question 4. What's the weather probably going to be like tonight?

Beth: Did you hear *that?* It's going to be really rainy and cold tonight.

Narrator: Conversation 5.

Ali: Maybe this is the night for us to stay in a motel.

Dan: I think so too. Camping's fun but not in the rain. Ah! We're almost in the town. Let's see if there's a motel.

Beth: Dan! Why didn't you stop?

Ali: Yeah! Didn't you see the sign? You could get a ticket!

Dan: No, I didn't! Sorry, guys!

Narrator: Question 5. Why is Dan sorry?

Beth: Whew! Be *careful,* Dan!

Dan: You're right. I didn't even *see* that stop sign.

5 Listening for Main Ideas page 190

Narrator: This is the capitol building for the state of Georgia. The capitol building is famous for its gold roof. The gold came from the mountains of Georgia.

Just east of the capitol building, in downtown Atlanta, is the Martin Luther King, Jr., National Historic Site. It's a memorial to Martin Luther King, Jr., the great leader of the American Civil Rights Movement. Martin Luther King, Jr., was from Atlanta. His grave is at this site.

Now we're just east of the city of Atlanta. This is Stone Mountain. It's a natural hill of stone. It's famous because a man carved an image of three Civil War generals on the side of the mountain. These generals are Jefferson Davis, Robert E. Lee, and Stonewall Jackson.

Now we're coming around to Interstate Highway I–20, to the west side of the city. This is Six Flags Amusement Park. It's a large amusement park with lots of roller coasters and other rides.

6 Listening for Places on a Map page 191

7 Listening for Details page 191

Narrator: Number 1.

Tour Guide: This is the capitol building for the state of Georgia. The capitol building is famous for its gold roof. The gold came from the mountains of Georgia.

Narrator: Number 2.

Tour Guide: Just east of the capitol building, in downtown Atlanta, is the Martin Luther King, Jr., National Historic Site. It's a memorial to Martin Luther King, Jr., the great leader of the American Civil Rights Movement. Martin Luther King, Jr., was from Atlanta. His grave is at this site.

Narrator: Number 3.

Tour Guide: Now we're just east of the city of Atlanta. This is Stone Mountain. It's a natural hill of stone. It's famous because a man carved an image of three Civil War generals on the side of the mountain. These generals are Jefferson Davis, Robert E. Lee, and Stonewall Jackson.

Narrator: Number 4.

Tour Guide: Now we're coming around to Interstate Highway I–20, to the west side of the city. This is Six Flags Amusement Park. It's a large amusement park with lots of roller coasters and other rides.

10 Listening for the Main Idea page 192

11 Listening for Specific Information page 193

Travel Agent: Yes, what can I do for you?

Alicia: I'd like to go to Walt Disney World, so I need information on flights to Florida.

Travel Agent: OK. I think I can get a good fare

for you to Orlando, Florida. Do you want to go first class, business class, or economy?

Alicia: Oh, economy, of course. I'd like the lowest fare you can find.

Travel Agent: All right. And that's one way or round trip?

Alicia: Round trip. I'd like to leave on Sunday the 12th and return on Saturday the 18th.

Travel Agent: Well, there's a very low fare on Sunday morning. It's only $145, but it's not direct. You have to change planes in Atlanta. There's a direct, nonstop flight, but the fare on that one is $680.

Alicia: That's OK. I'll change planes in Atlanta.

Travel Agent: OK. That's flight 690. It departs at 8:15 A.M. on Sunday the 12th and arrives in Orlando at 12:15.

Alicia: That sounds good.

Travel Agent: Oh, there's one more thing. It's a special low fare, so the ticket is nonrefundable.

Alicia: That's all right. I'm not going to change my plans.

Chapter 10 Our Planet

Part 1   Conversation: Earth Day

4 Listening for Main Ideas page 202

5 Listening for Specific Information (Part 1) page 202

6 Listening for Specific Information (Part 2) page 203

8 Listening for Stressed Words page 204

Alicia: Come in!

Lee: Hi, Alicia. How's it going?

Alicia: Hi, Lee. I'm fine . . . but busy!

Lee: What are you doing?

Alicia: I'm making a sign for Earth Day.

Lee: Earth Day? What's that?

Alicia: On Earth Day, people think about pollution and other problems with the environment.

Lee: Really! When is Earth Day?

Alicia: Next Monday.

Lee: . . . and is it every year?

Alicia: Yes, it is. The first Earth Day was in 1970, and it now happens every year, on April 22nd. On that day, people talk and learn about problems with the environment.

Lee: . . . like, how?

Alicia: Well, one year, thousands of people came to Washington, D.C., to support clean energy. In Italy, 150 towns and cities had Car-less Weekends when nobody could drive.

Lee: You mean Earth Day happens all over the world?

Alicia: Yes, it sure does! Earth Day happens in many countries.

Lee: And what's going on here at the college?

Alicia: There's a lot happening at the college. At the student union, there will be exhibits on pollution, . . . Students will also plant some trees around the college campus.

Lee: So what are you planning to do on Earth Day?

Alicia: I'm planning to give a speech about pollution. Also, I'm going to carry this sign.

Lee: What does it say? *Save the Earth!* That's great, Alicia. Can I go with you and help? I want to help the environment too.

Alicia: Sure, Lee. Would *you* like to carry a sign too?

Lee: Yes, I sure would!

Emphasis and Meaning page 205

Narrator: Conversation 1

Alicia: At the student union, there will be exhibits on pollution. Students will also plant some trees around the college campus.

Lee: So what are *you* going to do on Earth Day?

Alicia: I'm going to give a speech.

Narrator: Lee is asking about *Alicia's* plans compared to what other people do on Earth Day.

Narrator: Conversation 2

Alicia: I usually visit my family on special days like Thanksgiving and New Year's.

Lee: So what are you going to do for *Earth Day?*

Alicia: I'm going to give a speech at the student union.

Narrator: Lee is asking about Alicia's plans for *Earth Day* compared to other special days.

Narrator: Conversation 3

Alicia: I think about pollution on Earth Day, and I worry about the environment.

Lee: So what are you planning to *do* on Earth Day?

Alicia: I'm going to give a speech and carry a sign.

Narrator: Lee is asking about Alicia's *actions* compared to her thoughts.

9 Listening for Emphasis page 205

Narrator: Conversation 1

    Alicia: Some people think air pollution is a big problem, but others think progress is more important.

    Lee: Well, what do *you* think about pollution?

Narrator: Conversation 2

    Alicia: Air pollution and water pollution are two serious environmental problems.

    Lee: Do you think *air pollution* is the biggest problem?

Narrator: Conversation 3

    Alicia: One of the things I do on Earth Day is to stop driving my car.

    Lee: Will you ride your *bicycle* to school on Earth Day?

Narrator: Conversation 4

    Alicia: We're going to plant trees all over town on Earth Day. We have 500 trees to plant.

    Lee: How many trees will you plant on *campus?*

Narrator: Conversation 5

    Alicia: Students from the college are going to clean up Audubon Park, Haley Park, Finley Park, and Tom Lee Park.

    Lee: Which parks are *you* going to clean up?

Part 2 Using Language

1 Listening for Main Ideas page 208

2 Listening for Opinions page 208

Amy: Air pollution is so bad in this city! I think the local government should stop people from driving cars on certain days.

Nabil: You have a point. Air pollution *is* a problem, but not letting people drive on certain days is a bad idea. People need their cars to get to work, and trucks need to deliver goods to stores.

Amy: I'm afraid I don't agree with you there. Saving the environment is too important. People are so used to driving that they don't think of other ways to do things. If we stopped people from driving on certain days, maybe we could think of new ways to get around.

Nabil: I understand your point of view, but I still think it wouldn't be possible to stop people from driving.

Part 3 Listening

1 Using Context Clues page 210

Narrator: Speaker 1.

Speaker 1: In my opinion, it's very dangerous to walk on the streets at night. Someone might steal your money—or even hurt you. The police should do more to stop this problem.

Narrator: **Question 1.** What problem is Speaker 1 talking about?

Speaker 1: Because of crime, I'm afraid. I want to leave this city.

Narrator: Speaker 2.

Speaker 2: I agree that crime is a problem, but the problem with the air is even bigger. Every day, I look out the window, and the sky is brown and dirty. People shouldn't drive so much. And the factories should run in a cleaner way.

Narrator: **Question 2.** What does Speaker 2 think is a bigger problem than crime?

Speaker 2: Air pollution here is really bad. The city *must* do something to clean up the air.

Narrator: Speaker 3.

Speaker 3: I agree that crime and air pollution are serious problems. But we shouldn't forget what we have to drink. The rivers are dirty, the city water isn't safe, and I have to buy my water in bottles. Even the rain isn't good for the trees and plants.

Narrator: **Question 3.** What does Speaker 3 think is another serious problem?

Speaker 3: I think crime and air pollution *are* big problems, but water pollution is a big problem too.

Narrator: Speaker 4.

Speaker 4: I agree with Speakers 1, 2, and 3 that crime and pollution are serious in the city. But to me, just driving from one place to another is the most serious problem. I drive five miles to work, but it takes me half an hour because the traffic is so bad. Every year, there are more cars, trucks, and buses. Then when I go shopping, I have to wait in line for ten or twenty minutes just to pay! There are too few services for too many people.

Narrator: **Question 4.** What does Speaker 4 think is the most serious problem in the city?

Speaker 4: In my opinion, overcrowding is worse than crime and pollution.

Narrator: Speaker 5.

Speaker 5: It's good to talk about local problems, but I think it's important not to forget the big picture. The cities are only one part of a much bigger problem. We have to find answers to the biggest problem of all—protecting and preserving the earth.

Narrator: **Question 5.** What does Speaker 5 think is the biggest problem of all?

Speaker 5: In other words, we have to understand that problems aren't only in the cities but also in the whole environment.

4 Listening for the Main Idea (Part 1)
page 211

5 Listening for Main Ideas (Part 2)
page 211

6 Listening for Details page 211

Narrator: Message 1

It takes about 17 mature trees to clean the air of the pollution from one automobile. Give the trees a break on Earth Day and ride your bike or take a free shuttle bus to the Earth Fair in Marquette Park on Monday, April 22nd. Call 555-1234 for information.

Narrator: Message 2

What can you do to save the planet on Earth Day? Bring your recyclables to the Earth Fair recycling center at Marquette Park on Monday, April 22nd, from 10 A.M. to 5 P.M.

Narrator: Message 3

Less than one out of every quarter million slaughtered animals is tested for toxic chemical residues. On Earth Day, eat chemical-free treats at the natural foods area at the Earth Fair in Marquette Park on Monday, April 22nd.

Narrator: Message 4

A full gallon of water can run out of your faucet in less than sixty seconds! To celebrate Earth Day, turn off the water when you brush your teeth and come to the Earth Fair in Marquette Park on Monday, April 22nd.

Narrator: Message 5

One quarter-pound hamburger represents the killing of 55 square feet of rain forest, the loss of 10 pounds of topsoil, the use of 650 gallons of water, and the introduction of 500 pounds of carbon dioxide into the atmosphere. Save the planet and eat delicious veggie burgers at the natural foods area at the Earth Fair, Monday, April 22nd, at Marquette Park.

Vocabulary Index

CHAPTER 1

Are you kidding?
capital
divided
exact change
fare
good for
hometown
in advance
interesting
nightlife
pass
population
public transportation
seniors
ticket
transportation
zone

CHAPTER 2

a pair of (jeans)
brand
browse
crowded
deliver
favorite
fill out (a form)
furniture
gift
groceries
look around
look for (parking)
mall
No problem
on sale
online shopper
place an order
promise
purchase
save money/time/
    energy/gas
shipping
spend money/time

the best deal
the lowest/best/
    highest price
transaction
try (on)

CHAPTER 3

(be/get) homesick
    (for)
by mail/phone/email
call someone back
come by
expect someone
guess
leave a message
look forward to
    something
miss
miss a call
phone card
recognize
slender
stay/keep in touch
tall
wear glasses
What's the matter?

CHAPTER 4

(a) cold
(a) fever
(an illness) is going
    around
(dental) cleaning
(eye) exam
(the) flu
ache
angry
ankle
argument
aspirin
bandage
break (a leg)
cavity

checkup
cough
drugstore
emergency
flu
fluids
friends
hang up
headache
health clinic
ID card
insurance
    card/insurance
    number
make an appointment
medicine
menu options
prescription
press
sneeze
sprain (an ankle)
stay on the line
stolen
take your temperature
vomit

CHAPTER 5

(baseball) fan
accept an invitation
apologetic
ask (someone) out
bored
celebrate
cross-cultural
date
date/make a date
    (with someone)
excited
formal
get in
go out (with someone)
graduation party

have someone (over)
    for dinner
informal
invite someone (over)
look forward to
matchmaker
modern
permission
play (a game)
request
some other time
strict
student ticket
terrible
the favor of your
    presence

CHAPTER 6

advice
alert
can't keep one's eyes
    open
chemicals
complex
deprived
hardly
percent
research study
sleep in
sleep-deprived
solve
subject group
take a nap
wake up

CHAPTER 7

(one's) company
accurate
appointment
challenging
client
come up with
construction

discuss
Don't mention it
expenses
experience
find out
full-time
get out of
impressive
journalism
look for
once in a lifetime
part-time
presentation
public health
relatives
reporter
resume
rough
tired of
youth hostels

CHAPTER 8

an order of
beat
brown
calories
carrot
charge
cheese grater
chop
cucumber

decide
diet
good/bad for you
grate
hot tea
Italian dressing
maitre d'
mushroom
onion soup
order
ounce
picnic
produce
rice
teaspoon
thoroughly
tofu
vegetarian
worried about
You said it!

CHAPTER 9

advisory
arrive
business class
can't wait
change (a tire)
change planes
coach class
Couldn't we . . .

criminal
depart
direct
explore
first class
fishing equipment
flash flood
flat tire
freezing
I'd rather . . .
landmark
Let's
luggage
nonrefundable
nonstop
one way
one way (ticket)
prison
pull over
round trip
round trip (ticket)
should
skyline
sleeping bag
Sounds good/OK
spare tire
take up space
tent
the way back
tower
triangular

trunk
Wouldn't you
    rather . . .

CHAPTER 10

a lot going on
campus
carbon dioxide
endangered species
environment
exhibit
faucet
give a speech
mature
plant
pollute
pollution
recyclables
recycle
shuttle bus
slaughtered
student union
support
topsoil
toxic chemicals
veggie (vegetable or
    vegetarian)

Skills Index